Church IT:
Strategies and Solutions

NICK B. NICHOLAOU

A Church Law & Tax Resource
from Christianity Today

ChurchLaw&Tax

Published by Christianity Today International

christianitytoday.com

churchlawandtax.com

ISBN: 978-1-61407-918-7

Printed in the United States of America

DEDICATION

So many churches and ministries have invited me to help them over the last thirty years! I am thankful to each, and dedicate this book to The Bride of Christ, as well as to my amazing wife and daughter.

TABLE OF CONTENTS

FOREWORD

In the 1980s, I was privileged to lead what is now called Christian Camp and Conference Association. Back then, every camping leader was scrambling to ensure the computer age didn't leave them in the dust.

Most of us had a-friend-of-a-friend-of-Cousin-Eddie who gave us bad advice. I knew nothing, but I bought my first computer anyway—a Kaypro II. Few things in life are transformational. That machine was!

Fast forward to 1990 when I joined the management team at Willow Creek Community Church. The church had two IT guys then. The soft-spoken one installed a new computer in my office. With the bedside manner of a caring surgeon, he assured me my lack of technology savvy would not matter.

Gratefully, the church loaned us its IT team when we launched Willow Creek Association in 1992. We had an early version of an internal email system, but dozens of those pink "While You Were Out" phone message slips still ended up on my desk.

During a Chicago snowstorm in early 1994, a headhunter from sunny California called me about leading Christian Management Association (now called Christian Leadership Alliance). I called my wife from the office and when I arrived home that evening, she was packed!

I'm sharing all of this to say, with deep appreciation, that when I arrived in Southern California, Nick Nicholaou was there to assure me that IT would be the *least* of my worries at CMA. *He was right!*

Nick's amazing firm, Ministry Business Services Inc., ensured that CMA—while seeking to model God-honoring management practices to thousands of church and ministry leaders—would *also* walk the talk and employ God-honoring IT practices in our national office and in our national conferences.

As CMA's national section leader for IT, Nick's mind and heart created a ripple effect of Kingdom fruitfulness.

Malcolm Gladwell's bestseller, *Outliers: The Story of Success* notes the extraordinary power of the 10,000-hour rule. Gladwell would label Nick a "10,000-hour expert" based on the immense time Nick has invested with churches and ministries across the country. *He has seen it all—the good, the bad, and the ugly, yet he still has a contagious positivity about ministry.* Amazing!

So, without hesitation, I commend this very, very practical book to you. It is high time that a national leader elevated the foundational and critical work of IT! Nick gives you the information—and the why. His warm appreciation for the ministry of IT oozes out because of his high regard for the thousands of miracle-working IT people in the trenches.

So read and share this book with others: your pastor or boss, your colleagues, your volunteers, and your team members (if you have any!). Point out the helpful glossary in the back (a life-saver for me!) and the numerous resources.

When Rolla P. Huff was named president and CEO of EarthLink in 2007, *The Wall Street Journal* highlighted his priorities, which underlined the importance of an organization's operational side (including IT). Huff said,

> "It's all about execution.
> At the end of the day, I won't be judged
> on my plan as much as my execution."

Nick's insightful book will help you execute with excellence. And along the way, be sure to encourage and mentor others—like you—who are called by God to deploy the spiritual gift of administration.

JOHN PEARSON
Board Governance & Management Consultant
Author, *Mastering the Management Bucket*

INTRODUCTION

In my role as president of MBS, Inc. I've enjoyed the great privilege of serving churches as an IT consultant and strategist. I started in that role in 1987 and helped churches through a number of IT transitions, including answering these questions:

1. ***Should a church buy a computer?*** In 1987 churches wrestled through the concept of why a church would want a computer. At that time computers were very expensive, and owning one seemed eccentric! Very few churches had computers. A few subscribed to service bureaus, which is similar to today's hosted computing. Answering this question was my first area of focus in IT consulting, writing, and speaking.

2. ***Who on the church staff should have a computer?*** As churches began buying and using computers and saw how helpful they were, my next focus was to help them decide which church staff should get computers. Back then a basic desktop computer cost as much as $5,000! It became an issue of stewardship. For larger churches, giving computers to the finance department was a no-brainer; creating spreadsheets and the ability to automate check writing and contribution statements was easily justified. But what about other staff? Was giving them computers wasteful?

3. ***Why should computers be networked?*** Once churches began to recognize the value of using computers, many added computers for key staff. My next focus became the why's and how's of connecting computers together. The big question churches asked was, *Why would you want to connect these computers?* In the early days of networking there were so many new options and methods of connecting computers that it was a confusing choice. The strategic component of my work began to develop bigger muscles as I researched and determined what worked best and for the most reasonable cost. My focus was a mix of being practical and strategic, while balancing the budget sensitivities of churches.

4. ***Should a church be on the internet?*** When public access to the internet became available through the World Wide Web (www), churches wrestled with website and email issues—and this expanded my focus again. In the mid-1990s, Steve Hewitt, then Editor-in-Chief for *Christian Computing Magazine* (now *MinistryTech Magazine*) and I predicted there would come a day when you would see website addresses in television ads and on the sides of trucks! People were shocked and openly mocked *us*

5. ***What is virtualization, and should churches use that technology?*** When virtualization came along, my focus expanded again to include virtualized computers and servers. This technology saves so much money while increasing reliability and productivity, and improving disaster recovery!

6. ***Should churches use cloud technology?*** Around 2009,

I sensed that the Lord wanted me to strategically help churches move into the cloud. Just as he used me to help develop the *best practices* in each earlier phase of church computing, my impression was that he wanted me and my team to focus on helping bring churches into the cloud.

At each of these stages, the Lord gave me wisdom to identify good hardware, software, and platform strategies that were not biased toward any one vendor. He has given me the privilege of serving hundreds of churches directly and countless thousands indirectly through my writing and speaking at regional and national conferences.

The Purpose of This Book

This book is specific to IT in church and ministry environments. The church and ministry computing environment is unique. Through my work with churches, I have seen what churches do about IT issues that are not strategic. In the pages ahead, I address a number of the most common and costly IT mistakes churches make, with the hope that this book will help many church leaders think through better, more strategic approaches for applying computer technology to the mission of their churches—unique as their computing environments may be.

CHURCH IT'S MISSION

When you have vision,
it affects your attitude. Your
attitude is optimistic rather than
pessimistic. . . . This is nothing
more than having a strong belief
in the power of God; having
confidence in others around you
who are in similar battles with
you; and, yes, having confidence in
yourself, by the grace of God.

■

CHARLES R. SWINDOLL[1]

[1] Swindoll, C. (2007). *Dear Graduate: Letters of Wisdom from Charles R. Swindoll*. Nashville, TN: Thomas Nelson

IT DEPARTMENT STRUCTURE

> The work is too heavy for you;
> you cannot handle it alone.
>
> ■
>
> JETHRO, MOSES' FATHER-
> IN-LAW[2]

There are four different technology 'knowledge and skill' disciplines in most churches. Often church leadership thinks of them all as IT (Information Technology). That is probably because they all rely heavily on computer technology, and the assumption is that anyone involved in any of the four disciplines is equally capable of serving in any of the four areas.

However, each discipline uses different skills and tools. Unfortunately, churches often mistakenly group all four disciplines together into one "IT Department" and select a person strong in one of those disciplines to lead all four. It is one of the most common IT mistakes churches make.

---

[2] Exodus 18:18. The Holy Bible, New International Version (1984). International Bible Society

The Four Disciplines of Church Technology

The four disciplines are (1) web and graphic design; (2) audio/ video (A/V); (3) social media; and, (4) data infrastructure (the design and connecting of systems to ensure appropriate data flow at all levels). There are exceptions to each of these generalities. But the generalities also reveal some of the dominant characteristics of the people who specialize in each IT discipline.

1. **Web and Graphic Design.** Wikipedia describes this discipline as "the art of communication, stylizing, and problem-solving through the use of type, space and image."[3] It is similar to designing magazine ads that powerfully communicate a coordinated message all in one graphic, with the goal of moving the viewer toward an action. People who excel in this area are usually articulate communicators who are also very artistic. They use applications to draw, design, and do layout. They are often good project managers because of the timelines and project complexities involved in their work, but they are usually not highly skilled in A/V or data infrastructure, for instance.

2. **Audio and Video.** A/V people are also creative communicators. They specialize in cameras, projection systems, soundboards, lighting control boards, and storyboarding. Also good project managers, they can plan the A/V elements of a production from start to finish and make certain all is ready at showtime. The computers used to render videos require a lot of resources and are often more powerful than some servers!

---

[3] *https://en.wikipedia.org/wiki/Graphic_design*, accessed 8/8/2015

Because A/V people use high-quality computers and are usually articulate communicators, they are often tasked with IT oversight. But, like web and graphics people, they are usually not highly skilled in other technology disciplines.

3. ***Social Media.*** Social media people are gifted communicators. They are highly skilled at leveraging today's electronic communication mediums (Twitter, Instagram, Facebook, etc.) to begin and engage in conversations with a wide audience. Their tool is the written word, and although layout sometimes comes into play, they are usually not highly skilled in web and graphic design, A/V, or in the data infrastructure required to connect them with the world.

Jonathan Smith, Director of Technology at Faith Ministries in Lafayette, Indiana, said social media is often combined with web and graphic design or data infrastructure because people in those disciplines use social medial tools. But that often is a poor fit. It is best treated separately, he said.

4. ***Data Infrastructure.*** Infrastructure people are more like engineers than creative types, and they are often not very good communicators. Their personality tends to drive them toward analysis and the engineering of systems, where their focus is to make certain that data flows where it needs to go, whether that data is graphics, video, or data files (like spreadsheets). They tend to focus more on system designs, specs, and configurations, and are often not highly skilled in web and graphics, social media strategies, or A/V.

Which Discipline Is Best-suited to Oversee IT?

I'm an infrastructure guy, so my perspective may be a bit biased. However, here is what I see at many churches:

- When non-infrastructure people oversee IT, the infrastructure requirements necessary to support the needs of the entire church staff are often underestimated. This is usually because of an inadequate understanding of infrastructure engineering and strategy and is evidenced by the tendency towards non-enterprise hardware specs (meaning that the hardware chosen is usually not what corporations would consider appropriate to support high reliability needs with minimal cost). Less art than science, the data infrastructure discipline is more about engineering than creativity or communication.

- The infrastructure discipline is the foundational basis for all data transfer needs, so it usually is the best discipline to lead the technology needs of the church. However, two areas that infrastructure people struggle with are communication and an over-restrictive approach to policies. These weaknesses can erode their relationships with staff and leadership (more on this in Chapter 3). Over-restrictive policies also often prompt church staff to find workarounds, which can create numerous other risks and challenges.

Regardless of which discipline is responsible to lead a church's IT department, there are some things that can be done to improve it:

- If a non-infrastructure person leads the IT department, it is important to have a good and trusted infrastructure person in the department or to have a relationship with a good and trusted infrastructure consultancy. The infrastructure perspective is essential to having a system that works well for all staff and provides optimal and reliable transfer of every kind of data needed by the entire church team.

• If the IT department is led by an infrastructure person, that person should spend time getting to know the needs of the other three disciplines to make certain those needs are considered in the system design. They should also spend time with other church staff members and get to know their needs. In addition, the infrastructure person leading the department will need a champion at the church leadership level to help overcome the communication and policy challenges mentioned earlier.

Because an infrastructure person needs someone at the leadership level to help overcome communication challenges and implement policy changes, IT infrastructure is usually best placed under the chief operating officer (COO) or chief financial officer (CFO) of the church. Infrastructure is more of an operations discipline than it is a program discipline.

Communication Is Key

Many data infrastructure people struggle with communication. Jason Powell, though himself a skilled communicator as IT Director for Granger Community Church in Indiana, says it is helpful to have a great communication skills mentor. Granger's IT department is included as a part of its Communications Department, another good way to overcome the communications challenges.

David Brown, Technology Director for Capital Christian Center in Sacramento, California, agrees that communication is key: "The chasm between vision and reality can be filled with jagged rocks. There has to be a bridge-builder who can communicate effectively in both worlds. The tech world can be too black-

and-white or binary to communicate effectively to leadership. Being able to navigate necessary IT restrictions, while meeting the goals of leadership, will produce an outcome in which both sides are pleased."

2

WHO IS IT'S CUSTOMER?

> Be a yardstick of quality. Some people
> aren't used to an environment where
> excellence is expected.
>
> ■
>
> STEVE JOBS[4]

Many church team members complain that they feel like the IT Department is restricting them. When a staff member expresses a need to the IT Department, the first answer is often, "No, you can't do that." This is even true when leaders express a need! IT restricts what can be done on church computers. IT won't allow software purchases, offsite data access, and more.

Some polices need to be in place to protect the church, but many IT policies are not a good fit for how church teams work. The challenge of finding a way to both protect the church and empower the team deserves an appropriate balance.

---

[4] Young, J. (1988). *Steve Jobs: The Journey Is the Reward*. Glenview, IL: Scott, Foresman

Why Is IT So Restrictive?

The answer is primarily an issue of influence. Church IT tends to be restrictive because of other IT environments that IT staff have worked in or been influenced by. IT in for-profit companies, academic institutions, government agencies, and healthcare are all very restrictive, the latter two especially so. People working in church IT are heavily influenced by their frame of reference—or their consultants' frame of reference.

In non-church settings, IT security is often very high and employees are seen as a commodity. When a non-church IT department determines that a policy is important, violating that policy is grounds for termination.

Churches are different. Employees are not a commodity. Each employee—or *team member*—is someone we care about and for whom Christ died. In churches, we try to apply grace and mercy. And that can sometimes create a passive-aggressive culture where everyone perceives IT policies as nothing more than ineffective speed bumps that are okay to bypass—everyone, that is, except the IT department! This passive-aggressive culture can also frustrate staff who are uncomfortable with ignoring policies. The IT department can end up feeling unappreciated.

While consulting for a megachurch, I saw the passive-aggressive dynamic in an advanced state:

- The IT department was frustrated that the rest of the church staff seemed to ignore many IT policies in unforeseen and uncontrollable ways.

- Many on the church staff bragged to me about how they got around IT restrictions. Even top pastoral leaders in the church bragged about this. The executive pastor encouraged his team members to come up with ways to get past restrictive IT policies so they could get their job done!

• Some of the more compliant staff were frustrated on behalf of the IT department and could not understand why everyone treated IT so disrespectfully.

Who Is IT's Customer?

One of the best ways to overcome this common conflict is for the IT department to approach its role as though it is a for-profit business and every member of the church team is a customer.

Why does that help so much? A for-profit business knows it must meet its customers' needs effectively and in such a positive way that the customer will want to come back and give them more business. Anything less threatens a for-profit's very existence. Imagine the effect this underlying philosophy would have on most church IT departments—and on the church teams they serve!

That means IT must not dictate what people may or may not do on the system, *except when it is necessary to protect the team members and/or the organization.* Restrictive policies that are not truly necessary have the same effect as crying wolf when no wolf is there: people stop paying attention to the warnings. Thus, any restrictive policy needs to be carefully scrutinized to determine how essential it is before it's put into place. Top church leadership can help determine the validity of the policy and require buy-in from the team. Leadership's response and decision to enact the policy will become the force behind it rather than the force coming from the IT department.

Say "Yes" Whenever Possible

One year at a Church IT Network event, Clif Guy, Church of the Resurrection IT Director in Leawood, Kansas, told us about his IT team's astonishing approach to requests: His church IT department's policy is to say "yes" whenever possible. This approach is rare. But it is exactly the way IT should run in the church. The default posture always should be to say "yes!" That does not mean IT always says "yes" though. Sometimes the response really needs to be "no, and here's why." But having a "yes" default posture helps convey that IT is on the same team as the rest who are driven to fulfill their call.

Most church team members rarely understand the results of some IT-related decisions on overall productivity. IT needs to say "no" on occasion, but IT needs to say "no" so infrequently that when they do, the rest of the team will heed it.

Here's a Practical Example

One of the big debates at Church IT Network events is over something called "local admin." When setting up a team member's computer, the option exists to give that team member administrative authority over their computer. Doing so does not affect the security rights the team member will have on the network and its data, but only on the computer they use day in and day out. Because it only affects their computer, and not the overall system, it is referred to as local admin rights.

About half of church IT people believe in giving everyone local admin rights, and the other half adamantly oppose it. I am a big proponent of giving all team members local admin rights unless one of them proves they just cannot safely handle that much authority. Giving everyone local admin rights has some valuable benefits:

• It allows team members to install printer drivers, flash drive drivers, and so on, without having to contact the

IT department.

- It allows the user to run application updates and patches without the IT department's intervention.

- It dramatically reduces the number of support calls to the IT department, lowering the time—and potentially, staff—needed to handle the load of resolving all those support calls.

- It builds "customer" satisfaction.

However, there is a risk to giving everyone local admin rights. For example, a team member has the ability to load malware on their system or delete a necessary operating system file. After using this strategy on thousands of church computers for many years, I have found the risk to be minimal.

If your church grants local admin rights to all team members, IT needs to engineer ways to protect and resolve issues that could arise because of local admin rights. However, doing so is a significantly lower load and cost than *not* giving local admin rights. Here are some ways for IT to protect the system:

- Fully back up the church's data daily, and keep at least three to four weeks of those backups in case a problem isn't noticed right away.

- Make hard drive images of local computers using an app like Symantec's Ghost, so that, if necessary, reestablishing a computer's configuration can be quick and easy. This can be further simplified by buying similarly spec'd computers in bunches rather than individually, since all of the computers can be backed up by a single image.

If a team member proves repeatedly that they cannot be trusted with local admin rights, change only that team member's rights instead of restricting everyone on the team. This helps IT build a level of "customer satisfaction" that is a blessing for every member of the team.

3

LEADING IN AN IT VACUUM

> If it wasn't hard, everyone
> would do it. It's the *hard* that
> makes it great.
>
> ■
>
> TOM HANKS[5]

C hurch leadership makes decisions and sets direction for ministry programs, but usually without input or feedback from the IT department. Yet most decisions made today involve IT disciplines. Why does this happen? How do we reasonably overcome it?

The Challenge

Ministers, boards, and committees meet regularly to talk through the status of their church and identify strategic directions to increase their effectiveness in their communities,

---

[5] *A League of Their Own* [Motion picture]. (1992). USA: Columbia TriStar Home Video

among other things. These strategic directions might be about seasonal programming (Easter and Christmas, for example), group programming (young adults and families, for example), or community event involvement (such as a local parade). Each of these touch upon an IT discipline (graphics, A/V, social media, and/or infrastructure).

Unfortunately, IT leaders often learn of these programming plans late in the process.

Common examples I have seen in churches include:

- "I just found out that we're supposed to provide WiFi to the entire congregation in one week for something the pastor will do during his message."

- "We're supposed to provide check-in stations in a new part of the building and add a new kiosk in the lobby, but we don't have the bandwidth or connections in that part of the building or a secure connection in the lobby. I only have four days to make this work."

- "We added a pastor to the staff today, and we need to give this new pastor a computer."

I also receive calls about A/V and website issues. The problem in these examples is that IT wasn't told early enough to adequately prepare; yet they are responsible for making it happen! And the bulletin is already printed, so there's no way to adjust the schedule to allow for good preparation!

Very few churches and ministries include someone responsible for IT in the discussions and decisions for programming. Many churches see IT as operations overhead, so IT is not typically represented in those meetings.

The Consequences

Two common consequences of not having IT involved early enough in the planning process are:

1. Programming decisions are beyond the current ability of the church's IT disciplines to fulfill without expanding their hardware, software, or talent. This is not inherently negative, but it can be if the cost is higher than leadership anticipated.

   An example might be the decision to add financial transaction terminals to the campus (giving kiosks, credit card terminals, and so on). Even if credit and debit card numbers will not be maintained locally, transmitting these over the church's network and internet connection can trigger something called PCI Compliance, which can be very expensive depending on how the terminals are connected. Strategic implementation requires advance notice.

2. Expansion of IT hardware, software, or talent cannot be strategic if not given advance notice. I have seen many churches and ministries use hardware that is nowhere near "enterprise grade" quality. Instead, they have "consumer grade" solutions in place.

   Consumer grade solutions often get implemented because IT is up against a tight deadline and has to look for something—*anything!*—available in a store immediately. In Chapter 6 on "Rightsizing Hardware," I discuss the basis of one of my firm's catchphrases: "If you can find it on a shelf in a store, you do not want it!" When under a very tight, last-minute deadline, on-the-shelf consumer-grade solutions often offer the only hope of avoiding failure. The result is low-quality solutions, which cost more than appropriate solutions if given the appropriate time to order. From there, the problem persists because instead of replacing lower quality solutions once the deadline passes, the church keeps the consumer-grade solutions in place. That often translates into long-term reliance on solutions that have higher support costs, poorer performance, and lowers team productivity.

What Does Corporate America Do?

Larger companies often have a CXO position (this is a general reference to a top leadership level person where the X is a wildcard; Chief Executive Officer—CEO, Chief Operations Officer—COO, Chief Financial Officer—CFO, and so on) that is responsible for all things IT. Although many churches and ministries are smaller, we can still learn from this approach.

Many medium and larger corporations have a Chief Information Officer (CIO) or Chief Technology Officer (CTO) that participates in leadership meetings and on boards. These individuals help shape decisions so IT can get the right solutions in place to facilitate plans.

What Is a Reasonable *Church* Solution?

Adding a CIO or CTO to church leadership teams isn't the solution. Churches are focused on reaching the lost for Christ, and want as much of their budgets as possible to go toward programming rather than overhead.

IT usually reports to the CFO or COO of a church. That person often has the title of church administrator, church business manager, or executive pastor. Regardless of the title at your church, the person in that position needs to represent IT in leadership meetings in the same way a CIO or CTO would. The problem is that church CFOs and COOs usually don't know much about IT. That's okay if IT is managed strategically. I recommend the following:

- If leadership meetings happen regularly (weekly or monthly, for example), the CFO or COO should also have a regularly scheduled meeting with the IT person who reports to them to talk about the plans and directions that are being formulated in the leadership meetings *immediately* following the leadership meetings.

- If these follow-up meetings happen right on the heels of the leadership meetings, the leadership planning details will be fresh in the mind of the CFO or COO. He or she can then get the IT person's input, and relate any concerns to leadership within an appropriate timeframe. This can help leadership adjust planning if needed and gives IT notice of what may be coming so that IT can research and plan accordingly.

However, this is not an IT power grab! Rather, these meetings will help leadership accomplish plans for less money and will give IT enough advance notice to strategically research the appropriate enterprise-class solutions necessary for upcoming plans.

CHURCH IT SOLUTIONS

Computers allow us to squeeze the most out of everything.

■

BUZZ ALDRIN[6]

[6] Aldrin, B. (2012, August 3). Red Carpet News TV

4

SELECTING SOLUTIONS FOR THE WRONG REASON

> People say I make strange choices,
> but they're not strange for me.
>
> ◼
>
> JOHNNY DEPP[7]

When deciding how to meet a specific need, churches frequently ask other churches about solutions they used to meet that specific need. Whether it's hardware, software, or a database (such as Church Management Software), churches like to ask other churches what they use and whether they're happy with the choice to use it. That kind of research is good in theory but not in practice. It can have some significant downsides.

---

[7] Johnny Depp (2012, July 12). via Johnny Depp Fan Page in Facebook

The Quest to Be a Good Steward

Churches have IT budget constraints because they want as much of their budget as possible to go toward programming. So, the faster and more efficiently they can find operational solutions, the better. Right? Sometimes. Referrals from other churches can help us avoid mistakes, point us in directions that are good, or point us in directions that are bad.

Referral Request Assumptions

When we ask other churches for referrals of IT solutions, we make certain assumptions that may or may not be true. These assumptions are worth discussing. Following are two of the most significant:

- *Assumption 1:* "We are nearly identical. The other church is almost identical to ours in the way we do ministry, the things we value and prioritize, who we target in fulfilling our mission, the way our staffs are structured and work, and the way we minister to our congregation. Our two churches are nearly identical in personality, style, target, and focus."

- *Assumption 2:* "The other church researched its choice well. The other church did its due diligence in searching out the best possible solution based on its personality, style, target, and focus; its search was objective and exhaustive, landing on the best solution. In asking another church's leaders what they recommend, we save time and energy by not duplicating their research."

Problems with These Assumptions

With the first assumption, it is unlikely two churches are identical. Although many churches have similar goals of reaching the lost and helping them become true followers of Christ, the way each church accomplishes their goals is different. These differences are shaped by the personalities, education, skills, and gifting of the staffs. The mission of a church shapes it, affecting its strategies to reach people. The location, the surrounding community, and the physical layout of a church also shapes it. Each church has a unique personality, style, and culture—so unique, in fact, that it makes it unlikely two churches are identical.

That said, it is unlikely one church wants to do the exact same thing as the other. I frequently see this when churches are looking for a new ChMS (Church Management Software). When one church relies heavily on another church or individual's recommendation, the solution rarely lasts five years. The dissatisfaction is often expressed in statements like, "The software just doesn't match our church's ministry needs and style."

In the second assumption, the problem is that the referring church probably did not do an exhaustive search for the best solution to match their needs. Rather, they probably did the same thing you would like to do—call another church and ask them for a referral. If you trace the chain of referrals, you may find the first church that had chosen the solution many now are using because of their decision did so because of a discount made possible by a friend or a spouse, rather than the "best of class" solutions available. Even if that decision somehow worked out for the first church, it is unlikely the same solution will work for subsequent churches looking for guidance.

Ultimately, decisions made solely or based too heavily on the recommendation of another church are likely to fail.

A Better Way

The best method is to do an objective, exhaustive analysis using the unique needs of your church to decide what solution is best. However, this requires a significant investment of time, and someone to see it through.

The best way to determine your church's needs is through surveys and/or interviews with your team members most affected by the solution. The key to success is to do this phase of research without an agenda favoring any of the ministries at your church.

From there, all solutions should be reviewed to determine which one best matches your church's needs.

My method is a bit more *old school*. I interview each team member (sometimes in individual interviews and sometimes in focus group interviews). In each interview, I first establish the person's role so I understand that person's perspective. Then I ask a few questions:

- What software and hardware do you use in your job?

- What tasks does the system do for you now that you consider crucial?

- What does the system do that slows you down or gets in the way?

- How could the system serve you better?

- What else would you like the system do for you?

You may notice I never ask what solution they wish they had! The interviews are to identify needs to help find the best solution.

I ask these in interviews (instead of a questionnaire) because some of the answers lead to follow-up questions that glean information I would otherwise never get. Then I compile a survey (customized and built on previous surveys—more than 30 pages long) to send to all ChMS providers to help determine which can meet the church's needs. I also send a modified copy to the team members so they can weight each item on the survey, with choices of unimportant, might be nice, important, essential, or no opinion. I multiply the numeric values of the results of both groups to get an objective score for the providers most likely to meet the church team members' needs well.

Once you have objectively identified the top three solutions, you and your team should schedule live demos or visit other churches using them. This step helps your team members determine whether the solutions are good to use the way they would want to use them.

By involving your larger church team in the process, you will also help overcome one of the chief complaints of church staff. According to Chuck Lawless,[8] staff members often feel excluded from decision-making processes, making them feel they have no voice—that their opinions do not matter.

Giving your team a voice in the process takes more time and energy, but it increases team buy-in, encourages team members that their opinions are valued, and gets everyone focused on the positive aspects of the selected solution.

Do Your Research. It's Worth the Effort!

Many times quick decisions are made because such-and-such church uses a particular solution. Checking with other churches can help shorten the list of preferred solution providers, but don't

---

[8] Lawless, C. (2015, March 24). 12 Frequent Burdens of Church Staff. *ManagingYourChurch.com*

make the decision solely based on those recommendations. Still do the research with your staff (they will thank you!). Gather a list of criteria to use in the decision-making process, and still require live demos, or visit churches with the solution in place to see if it will fit your church's culture.

5

CHURCH MANAGEMENT SOFTWARE (ChMS)

> What turns me on about the digital
> age, what excites me personally,
> is that you have closed the gap
> between dreaming and doing.
>
> ∎
>
> BONO[9]

Using computers in churches is different from most settings. How IT departments in churches serve their "customers" and some of the solutions churches use are also different.

In the mid-1980s, I did my first exhaustive study on the software used by churches to manage financial and non-financial data. At that time, there were 262 solutions available to help in these vital areas! I established some reasonable minimal criteria

---

[9] Bono, P. (2005) TED Conference

for review, and only 17 made it through that filter! That meant there were many inadequate solutions. Because there were so many to choose from, it was nearly impossible for a church to do a good and thorough analysis.

Since those early days of church computing many solution providers have merged, consolidated, or gone out of business. Many new solutions have sprung up, too!

We collectively refer to these solutions as ChMS solutions. Today there are about 75 viable solutions written for churches and marketed to help them in these areas.

Why ChMS Instead of More General Solutions?

The financial and non-financial needs of churches are unique and not easily met with non-ChMS solutions.

In the financial area:

- Church accounting systems need to track various income and expense transactions, many of which close to different "capital"-equivalent accounts that are restricted (temporarily or permanently) or unrestricted. This is an accounting issue that sets church accounting needs apart from most other organizations:

  - Income and expense accounts close to a capital account—in companies it might be retained earnings; in churches it is a fund balance, also referred to as a net asset.

  - The unique aspect of nonprofit accounting is that income and expense accounts tied to various purposes and funds (like the missionary fund, the building fund, and so on) need to close to those various fund balance accounts and produce an available balance of how much is in each fund being tracked.

This helps fulfill one of the unique responsibilities churches have in their accounting systems, which, according to ECFA President Dan Busby, is "using the gifts within the limits of the donor's restrictions. To accomplish this, churches must have accounting systems which not only track restricted gifts in the donor management system, but also track the expenditure of the funds and unused funds (temporarily restricted net assets)."[10]

- Many churches keep their books on a "cash basis" or "modified cash basis," with only a small percentage of churches on the "accrual basis." A ChMS solution needs to accommodate all three. (Modified cash is a mixture of the cash and accrual methods in which only some items, accounts payable, for example, are managed on a cash basis.)

- There are unique aspects to managing payroll in churches. For example, ministers' income may or may not be subject to income tax withholding. The housing allowance portion of their income needs to be tracked as federally non-taxable, and none of their income is subject to FICA withholding.

In the non-financial area:

- Churches track all kinds of demographic and contact

---

[10] Busby, D. (2015) Four Accounting Challenges for Churches. *www.ecfa.org/Content/Four-Accounting-Challenges-for-Churches*

information. That's not uncommon among CRM (Customer Relationship Management) solutions. What makes it much more complex in churches are the life events and family/extended-family relationships that need to be tracked.

- An important database function in many churches is the ability to securely check children in and out for children's ministry events, such as Sunday school. In addition to the checking in and out process, churches need to track allergies, restraining orders, restricted access, and many other pieces of data that keep children safe—and help parents feel their children are safe.

- Tracking attendance helps identify those who may need some follow-up and encouragement.

- Tracking contributions and pledges is essential. This feature is normally considered a ChMS non-financial feature because many solution providers do not offer their own accounting solution, but all need to offer contributions tracking. There are specific legal requirements that allow contributors to write-off their contributions at tax time that these systems must satisfy.

Why Not Create Your Own Software Solution?

Many churches and ministries have gone the route of creating their own software solution. It rarely works for these reasons:

- *It will never be completed.* The process of creating your own software solution begins with gathering a list of needs, and then creating the software solution to meet those needs. After writing it, the testing begins, followed by fixes. Then more testing happens, and then, hopefully, it is released for use. To get to a release date takes a lot of time, energy, and focus. As users begin to use the new custom solution, the list of needs will expand beyond the original list. Then more work begins to release version 2, version 3, and so on. Buying a full-featured ChMS means that most of what the church team wants will be included because of the solution provider's experience with so many other customers. Implementation also will happen much faster in comparison.

- *It will be difficult to support.* Every software solution requires support, which requires someone to support it. Then, when underlying operating system (OS) updates are released (like Windows or Mac OSX), the solution needs to be tested and modified based on those new OS requirements. In addition, we all eventually move on, either geographically or because our life's time has ended. When that happens, the church will need to find someone who can take responsibility for the custom solution, further develop it, and support it. Finally, because of the time and work involved, it's unlikely the process will be well-documented, meaning subsequent developers and staff members will struggle using it.

- *It will be **very expensive**.* The amount of time spent to develop, implement, support, and upgrade the solution will be very expensive. Add to that the cost of lost staff productivity while the solution is tested and enhanced. It is a very expensive proposition; one I very rarely recommend.

I write an annual article that lists the current providers of ChMS solutions, published at the end of each year by The Church Network.[11] I also post a free copy of it on my firm's website (*http://www.mbsinc.com/church-donor-management-software-chms/*).

Reasonable Expectations

Churches and ministries often ask me to help them look for new ChMS database and accounting systems. During those conversations, I talk through what their team can expect from whatever new solution they choose. Most people don't realize what "there is no perfect solution" truly means. The very best anyone can expect is an 80-85 percent expectation match, or match of solution features to the needs of any church or ministry. Stated from the other side of that equation, the best they can hope for is a 15-20 percent set of missed expectations.

If a church already has a top-tier solution, the process of searching for and transitioning to a new solution may be nothing more than trading one 20% set of missed expectations for a different set of 20% missed expectations. If that's true, then that church may be better off exploring other ways to overcome their dissatisfaction before starting the transition journey. I'll address this further in Chapter 12.

---

11 The Church Network: *http://www.nacba.net/Pages/Home.aspx*

6

RIGHTSIZING HARDWARE

It is far more important to be able to hit the target than it is to haggle over who makes a weapon or who pulls a trigger.

■

DWIGHT D. EISENHOWER[12]

One of the most common mistakes churches and ministries make is related to the hardware they buy. I can say this objectively because my firm does not sell or profit from the hardware or software our clients purchase. Hardware and software sales have never been in our game plan.

The mistake manifests itself in three ways:

- Incredible overspending on highly sophisticated hardware the church will never take advantage of (overbuying),

---

[12] Eisenhower, D. (1958, April 17). Address to the American Society of Newspaper Editors and the International Press Institute

- Buying consumer grade hardware that doesn't work very well in a corporate network setting (underbuying), and

- Buying hardware built locally.

In each of these mistakes, the church usually spends more on its purchases than necessary, either in outright purchase costs or in higher support costs and lost staff productivity.

Our firm works hard to stay neutral with hardware, software, and platforms so we can effectively evaluate the options in the marketplace and make appropriate recommendations to our clients. This chapter reflects that neutrality.

Overbuying

Most vendors do not understand the needs of churches, and thus have a difficult time making appropriate recommendations. Some overestimate the church's needs, recommending hardware with sophisticated features the church will never use.

Overbuying is often the result of one of three things:

1. *Buying based on possible future needs.* Many churches think somewhat evangelistically when expressing their growing technology needs. But if needs don't materialize for three or four years, the result will be overbuying.

2. *Recommendations based on limited understanding.* Churches are unique in their hardware needs. If the church trusts someone's 'counsel' who has limited perspective (someone whose IT expertise is focused in another industry), the result will often be overbuying.

3. *Vendor recommendations that affect the vendor's*

profit. My firm has been to many churches that previously used IT vendors who sold churches hardware based on what they made, sold, or had in stock, but the hardware didn't come close to meeting the church's needs. It could be due to the reason mentioned above—where a member of the congregation worked for the company. In many cases, my firm has concluded that overbuying was because of the impact sales had on the vendor's bottom line.

The most common example of overbuying I see is Cisco firewalls and switches. These powerful, feature-rich solutions can almost definitely meet any church's needs. In fact, they significantly *exceed* the needs of most churches! The problem is that the features of Cisco firewalls and switches require a deep understanding of IT communication technology, and so their configuration and maintenance require a Cisco-certified engineer. That is expensive! And those higher-end features rarely benefit churches and ministries.

A church recently needed a local area network (LAN) revamp because its current configuration wasn't meeting its needs. When looking at their server configuration, my firm discovered it surpassed many servers found in high-end datacenters! The church spent more than twice what it needed on that server, and the church would never come close to taking advantage of its huge processor, RAM, and storage capacities.

Underbuying

Many churches and ministries mistakenly buy their computers from stores like Best Buy, Staples, or Costco. Many IT professionals have a saying in common: *If you can find what you need on a shelf in a store, you don't want it.* That goes for computers, printers, switches, and more.

There are differences between enterprise-spec systems and consumer-grade systems. Here are a couple that are not readily apparent:

- The engineering and match-up of components are at a higher level in enterprise systems than are usually found in consumer-grade systems. What many don't realize is that most computer components for both specs (consumer and enterprise) are manufactured on the same assembly line or process. The components are tested after being manufactured, and depending on how they score in testing, their test (or performance results) will determine their model number and associated cost. Thus, similar-looking components can be in both systems, but they will perform very differently. Enterprise-spec systems usually include higher-rated components, and have a higher level of research and development (R&D) invested in them by the company whose name is on the product (Dell, HP, and so on).

- Consumer-grade computers usually have a lot of trialware (software you get to try before you buy, but probably don't want). The Companies offer trialware to try to influence you to buy their software after trying it. This approach helps underwrite the cost of the computer, which lowers its purchase price. Trialware usually means a less-efficient user experience, and less-efficient user experiences translate to wasted time.

  Another problem with trialware is that it often doesn't uninstall completely. The little bits and pieces left behind can sometimes be the cause of problems that users later encounter.

Underbuying is often the result of having to buy something fast because there wasn't a strategy in place to anticipate needs and allow purchases to be planned. Planned purchases usually mean better stewardship because they allow time for ordering enterprise-spec systems at the lowest possible cost. Enterprise-spec systems don't necessarily cost a lot more; they're just better in an enterprise (non-consumer) environment where systems are networked.

Buying Locally Built Systems

In the early days of personal computers, many people thought buying locally built computers was best. They thought the support would be better since they were built nearby. Maybe in the 1980s that was sometimes true, but more often *locally built systems need more support* because they do not have the benefit of the level of R&D a larger company, like Dell or HP, could invest in them. Even consumer-class systems have some R&D. But locally built systems are only assembled. A local shop may do its best to buy great components, but local shops have limited opportunity or capability to test how each of those components work together. Local shops certainly do not have the buying power to request manufacturer firmware changes to components that would improve the way their component interacts with other selected components.

Surprisingly, some churches still buy locally built systems! There is no way a local shop can compete with the quality, reliability, and support of a well-engineered system.

So buy right! Buy enterprise systems for your church or ministry. You will save in the end.

7

VIRTUAL COMPUTERS

> It's better to be a fake somebody
> than a real nobody.
>
> ■
>
> MATT DAMON[13]

I n the late 1990s, a technology was introduced into modern
computing that existed previously only on large mainframe
and midrange computers. That technology, called *virtualization*,
made it possible for a computer or server to concurrently run
multiple computers—*on one device!*

At first, I was skeptical. How would it affect performance
and reliability? And why would anyone want to do such a thing?

Many churches ask the same questions—if they are even
aware of this technology. At national and regional conferences
when I ask for a show of hands, rarely do even 25 percent of
church leaders indicate they have virtualized servers.

---

[13] *The Talented Mr. Ripley* [Motion picture]. (1993). USA: Miramax Films

This technology can save churches a lot of money, improve network reliability, and improve network administration. And it's free! Well, free for most churches, anyway; more on that in a bit.

How Does Virtualization Work?

Virtualization requires an app called a *hypervisor*, which functions like a shim or wedge between the bare hardware and the Operating System (like Windows, Mac OSX, or Linux). Rather than installing the OS directly onto the computer or server, the hypervisor is installed first. Once it is installed, a wizard then helps you install as many virtual computers onto the physical computer or server as it has resources (processors, RAM, storage, and so on) to host! Thus, the physical computer is often referred to as a host. To help explain how this works, the steps to creating a host and the computers and servers that will run on it are:

1. Install the hypervisor.

2. Use the hypervisor's wizard, or menu, to say you want to create a virtual computer or server. Answer the hypervisors questions about:

   a. How many processors do you want the virtual system to have?

   b. How much RAM do you want the virtual system to have?

   c. How much storage (hard drive size) do you want the virtual system to have?

3. The hypervisor then takes a few minutes to create the virtual computer as you've spec'd it *logically* (vs *physically*). Once it's done, it will tell you to insert the OS installation media (like inserting a DVD or pointing to an iso file[14]). From that point forward, it looks like you're doing a normal OS installation, except that it's running in a window because it is a *virtual* computer!

Depending on how much physical resources the host has, you can install many virtual computers and servers. In my firm's datacenter, we run dozens on a single host!

Why Would You Want a Virtual Computer?

Physical computers and servers cost a lot of money. The surprising thing about them, though, is that for the most part, their physical resources go largely unused. For instance, if you were to monitor the processor's activity level in a server after it starts up, you'd find that it rarely goes above 10 percent utilization. The processor is the most expensive component in the machine, and yet most of the time it is idle! The same is true for many other resources. Virtualization helps maximize the return on investment made when purchasing that machine.

When I first began working with virtual servers and computers, I was skeptical a virtual server could deliver the high degree of reliability churches need. I learned a properly configured one could.

One of the reasons virtualization improves reliability is that the best way to set up network servers is to do so with each major separate network service having its own server.

---

[14] An iso file is an image of a CD or DVD that can be mounted logically just as though it was physical media. You can also burn an iso file to optical media and run it that way.

So, an email server should run on its own server, as should a database server, file server, endpoint server, and so on. That means the best reliability requires many servers. That strategy would be out of reach for most church budgets were it not for virtualization.

With virtualization, you can have a couple of physical servers—or hosts—provide the resources for many virtual servers. That amounts to large savings—with improved reliability. A win-win!

Brands and Costs of Hypervisors

There are three main players in the hypervisor marketplace: VMware's ESXi, Microsoft's HyperV, and Citrix's XenServer. VMware pioneered the technology, and its solution is currently the most mature, powerful, and easiest to use. HyperV is growing in its abilities, but ESXi still has the edge. Since both HyperV and ESXi are free, I recommend going with ESXi.

Hypervisors typically are free for most churches. The reason is that these companies make their income based on tools and features that only large organizations need. The best way to tell if you need those features is whether your organization uses a SAN (Storage Area Network) on the network. SANs are very expensive devices, usually costing more than $25,000. If you have a SAN, you know it, and the relatively small cost of the hypervisors features you would want would be a slam-dunk decision to purchase.

Most churches do not have a SAN. That means the basic set of features included in the free hypervisor should take care of your needs!

The Bottom Line

The bottom line on virtualization for any church with one

or more on-site servers is that if your church hasn't already, it most likely should be taking advantage of the power and reliability virtualization can add to your network. The price tag is certainly no barrier for doing so!

8

SOFTWARE CHARITY LICENSING

> I was called to do this, and when you are called to do something you don't give up. If you believe in something strongly enough, you continue to push until you find a way to make it work.
>
> ■
>
> CHRIS BOOTH[15]

In the early 1990s, Chris Booth and I (and I'm certain there were others, too) independently lobbied solution providers to offer licensing discounts to churches similar to those available to academic organizations and government agencies. The first large provider to agree to my request was Novell, a company that pioneered the software that made standardized local area networks possible. Then, mostly due to Chris' efforts, the second was WordPerfect, the pioneer for word processing

---

[15] Roberts, L. (2008, November 28). A Higher Calling: Chris Booth gave up corporate life to bring bargain high-tech supplies, services to nonprofit organizations. The Journal Times

software. Microsoft was third. (Microsoft eventually won both of those software categories due to its code development focus and market strategy.)

Today, many solution providers offer charity licensing discounts at, or near to, academic licensing discounts. Surprisingly, I still meet many in ministry that are unaware of these terrific discounts! Thus, they unnecessarily overspend on software.

Why Are Charity Discounts Offered?

Discounts are a great way for solution providers to offer philanthropic assistance to organizations that help society, but there is also a solid business case for doing so!

Board members and many other volunteers run churches and ministries. Many of those are decision makers or decision influencers in their paid jobs. Their hearts are definitely tied to helping the churches they serve to be effective.

These same volunteers and board members, often in an effort to increase effectiveness at a reasonable cost for church computing, end up championing the same solutions at their paid jobs. Discounts to churches and ministries make for very inexpensive marketing for the solution providers!

Lee Iacocca, an auto industry leader who helped run Ford Motor Company and eventually turned Chrysler around from near bankruptcy, used a similar strategy. It was one of his many successes. In his autobiography,[16] he said the challenge in the auto industry was to find new ways to get folks to do a test drive in their cars. When he realized that in the car rental industry people were actually *paying* to test drive cars, he made selling new cars at a low price to rental car companies a priority that translated into many test drives!

---

[16] Iacocca, L. (1984). *Iacocca An Autobiography*. Toronto: Bantam

Where Can You Get Charity License Pricing?

Many sellers of software have the ability to sell charity licenses. The key is to ask your software solution seller to make certain they are using charity-licensing SKUs when selling you software. If you're not certain that you are being offered true charity licensing, check with the solution provider (Microsoft, VMware, and so on). If a solution you want to use doesn't offer charity-licensing discounts, ask them if they'd be willing to extend their academic licensing discount to your organization. Really, it is in their best interest to do so. Don't pay full retail because doing so is usually not necessary for a charity.

Charity Licensing Pitfalls

A few companies are changing the way they offer charity-licensing agreements, and it involves a danger for many churches and ministries. These solution providers are including social engineering restrictions in the charity license, which go against many church and ministry doctrines. Avoiding those licensing agreements may be in your organization's best interest.

The two most prominent solution providers doing this are Google and Microsoft. Both do it exclusively with their online solution charity-licensing agreements, but not with their academic licensing agreements. In Microsoft's case, it also is not doing this with its Volume License Agreement (VLA), charity-licensing agreement.

In the charity-licensing agreement for Google Apps, charities are required to certify they do not discriminate in hiring or in employment practices related to the LGBT (Lesbian, Gay, Bi-Sexual, and Transgendered) community in any way. Microsoft's Office 365 charity license is similar, though we recently had success in getting them to add a statement and an FAQ explaining that churches and religious organizations may not be required to do so based on the laws that govern them and allow certain types of discrimination.

So Microsoft is making room for churches and ministries in their license agreements. Google, however, is not. And this is not a legal issue (though it could impact a legal proceeding); it is a mechanism Google is using to filter which organizations they want to donate their software to. Falsely certifying that an organization does not discriminate in its employment practices regarding LGBT issues, then, is taking from Google what they do not want to give.

In raising this concern, I am not taking the position that this should or should not be an issue. Christian churches and ministries love individuals in the LGBT communities. They want to serve them by introducing them to Christ and helping them grow in their relationship with him—a value-changing relationship! However, for many organizations, the employment practices requirement in the agreements pose a problem. It's important that churches and ministries are aware of these restrictions. Just as I was involved in lobbying for charity discounts so many years ago, I am hoping to help remove this language from these licenses.

Don't Be Afraid of Hearing "No"

Many years ago I read a book on negotiating that said most people don't ask for concessions when they have an opportunity to negotiate because they're afraid of a "no" response. That affected me, and I began asking for concessions more often than I did previously. Sometimes I get the "no" response, but many times, I get a "yes" if the request is reasonable. So, if your software solution provider does not offer charity-licensing discounts yet, ask for it. The worst the provider can say is "no"!

9

MAKING WIFI WORK!

> Whenever you find yourself on the side of the majority, it is time to reform.
>
> ■
>
> MARK TWAIN[17]

Many churches today broadcast WiFi on their campus for the convenience of staff and guests. WiFi seems to behave mysteriously, though, and only a small percentage of churches are completely pleased with how their WiFi works. There are reasons (largely hardware spec related), and there are strategies that every church would be wise to have in place to protect the church and those who use its WiFi.

Can WiFi Be Reliable?

The short answer is yes, but the long answer is *yes, if you understand how it works and engineer accordingly.* The problems

---

[17] Twain, M. (1878). *Mark Twain at Large.* Henry Regnery Co.

many experience with their campus WiFi deployments are fairly predictable, and easily avoided.

The most common WiFi problems we hear from churches include:

- **People can't get a connection.** This is most often a hardware spec problem. The cause is usually from using consumer-spec WiFi access points (WAPs), which directly relates to the discussion in the Underbuying section of Chapter 6 (see page 49). The WAPs you can buy off-the-shelf usually have a limit of about 25 connections. Some think that buying a bunch of them will overcome that limitation, but it doesn't.

- **The WiFi is too slow and devices drop their connection.** WAPs broadcast their signal over channels that, if not managed, bleed over and interfere with each other. Also, few routers or firewalls have the appropriate specs to accommodate the large burst of internet traffic that happens during church services and programs.

- **People can access content we don't want them accessing.** WAPs that are simply plugged into church network switches or routers can allow access to the internal network systems (like servers and printers) and to inappropriate websites. They need to be managed by the firewall, something few off-the-shelf WAPs can accommodate.

Hardware

Off-the-shelf WAPs have a limit of about 25 connections that can connect to them at a time. Buying ten of them does not increase the capacity to 250 as you'd anticipate. The problem is that their hardware doesn't have the feature set necessary to allow them to work together. Instead, they conflict with each other and even interfere with each other.

My firm learned this the hard way and recommend WAPs designed to operate in a commercial environment. We prefer Ruckus WAPs. Ruckus has WAPs that can accommodate as many as 500 or more connections and can coordinate with each other when there are multiple WAPs deployed on a campus!

The next part of the solution is the firewall. In Chapter 16, I explain why we recommend SonicWALL firewalls. The key to a good WiFi system is that the firewall needs to be able to handle the volume of internet traffic during church services and programs. Few off-the-shelf units have what's needed.

The firewall also helps protect those connected to the church's WiFi from websites that have inappropriate content. This is essential—especially if children might be connecting to the internet.

Configuration

When you search for a WiFi signal with a device you'd like to connect (smartphone, tablet, computer, etc.), you see a listing of names. Those names are Service Set Identifiers, or SSIDs. We typically configure three SSIDs for churches. These are managed in the firewall, and are an important part of a good WiFi strategy.

The three SSIDs we usually configure for our clients are:

1. *Guest.* This SSID only has access to the internet, and that access is filtered to prevent adult-oriented website access.

2. *Lay.* This SSID is similar to the Guest SSID, but is password protected and has protected bandwidth to accommodate lay leaders who need access to YouTube or

other similar streaming content while teaching a class. It also might include access to a printer to accommodate printing speaker notes or handouts.

3. *Staff.* This SSID is password protected and may even be hidden![18] It's only for church staff and includes access to the internet and to network servers and devices.

WiFi Security

Churches should protect access to their WiFi system by password protecting each SSID.

A church in Missouri learned the hard way that open and un-protected WiFi can cause significant problems. The church's WiFi was not protected with a password and it ran 24/7. Someone was driving into their parking lot after hours, connecting to their WiFi from the parking lot, and distributing child pornography.

When the FBI investigated, the church experienced two problems:

1. The FBI confiscated the church's computers—*all* of them, including the servers! They confiscated them because they are required to do a forensic examination to determine if any were involved in the distribution of child pornography. The church was without their computers for some time, which would cause problems for any church due to the dependence on computers for operations, study prep, and so on.

2. The story hit the news in a big way—television and newspapers. A headline in one newspaper was "Child

---

[18] It is possible to hide an SSID so only those who need it even know it exists.

porn investigation focused on [the church name]".
A television news report was titled "Child porn linked to church IP address." You can imagine how this bad press impacted the church, and how long it would take to recover from the impact.

Most churches, in the name of being a *welcoming church*, don't want to password protect their guest WiFi. For our clients who make that choice, we recommend—at a minimum—they turn off their SSIDs that are not password protected when no church service or program is running. That's only possible (without manually unplugging all WAPs) if the church is running an enterprise-class solution like the one my firm recommends (SonicWALL firewall with Ruckus WAPs).

Taking Security a Step Further

A vulnerability I see at many organizations—not just churches—is device default passwords still active. This applies to WAPs, but it applies to other IT devices too. A good practice is to always replace the default password on *any* IT device.

Gary Messmer, my firm's lead engineer, while visiting his auto dealership for routine car maintenance, looked to see if there was a WiFi signal (SSID) he could use. He found one, but it was password protected. The SSID was the default name assigned to their WAP by the consumer-class manufacturer that named the WAP's manufacturer and model! Being familiar with those devices, he decided to try the default password. He was in! He connected to the dealership's database and pulled up someone's record, walked over to the service manager, and while showing him his computer screen asked, "Is this your dealership database?" The service manager was shocked!

In Chapter 16, I discuss why churches need to be proactive

about managing their IT security. All data is vulnerable, but in the church we need to make certain we are doing our due diligence to protect our data and the information that could hurt someone if it were inappropriately accessed.

10

VoIP vs. TRADITIONAL PHONE SYSTEMS

> The overall point is that new technology will not necessarily replace old technology, but it will date it. By definition, eventually, it will replace it.
>
> ■
>
> STEVE JOBS[19]

Several years ago, I decided my firm needed a new phone system. Our system at that time was a peer-to-peer system, and it was significantly limited.

Our Challenge

When looking at our options, I was concerned with the prices normally associated with new phone systems. Typical PBX phone systems (Private Branch Exchange, typified by having an operator or receptionist) can cost tens of thousands of dollars!

To serve churches and ministries well, my firm runs on a very thin margin, so I didn't want to spend unnecessarily. I

---

[19] Jobs, S. (2011). *Steve Jobs: His Own Words and Wisdom.* Cupertino Silicon Valley Press

decided to look for something less traditional that wouldn't cost as much. Many churches also operate on thin margins; and I realized that what we discovered will be useful to churches as well.

Initially, the solution to my quest seemed to be VoIP (Voice over Internet Protocol), but even many of those systems cost more than $10,000. At a Church IT Network event I attended around that time, a number of attendees talked about a free PBX server that could run as a virtual server. I was leery because "free" is often more expensive than it's really worth. But considering the expense of the alternative, I decided to research this further and give it a try.

There are two aspects to VoIP.

1. Connecting your building to the world telephone system via VoIP technology vs standard phone line technology.

   - This is what most people think of when they think of a VoIP system.

   - Standard phone lines are costly, and VoIP connections can save you significant money!

   - The vendor we prefer for VoIP connections is *Bandwidth.com*. They provide their SIP trunks to churches for a significant discount!

     - Metered lines (no free long distance or toll calls) for $15.00/month per trunk. Long distance and toll calls bill at less than 2¢ per minute.

- Unmetered lines (long distance and toll calls included) for $22.50/month.

- I recommend churches get the metered lines since it would take more than 6 hours per month per trunk to get the metered cost up to the unmetered cost.

- VoIP SIP trunks save churches money every month!

2. The internal corporate phone system, known as a PBX, that connects church team members via extensions.

PBX Technology

Many sources I read said that because PBX technology is very mature (dating back to the days of switchboard operators using cables to connect calls, and even though technology has evolved and those manual technologies were replaced, the term PBX is still used), there were now a number of free open source PBXes available that are solid. Most recommended the same one mentioned at the Church IT Network event, so I decided to test it to see if it was as good as suggested.

My firm downloaded a solution called Asterisk and configured it as a virtual server on one of our hosts. We found it solid but challenging. A colleague who works on VoIP PBX systems recommended we switch to a version of the same solution called *FreePBX*. He said it was based on *Asterisk*, but with more features and a better graphical user interface (GUI). We switched and haven't looked back!

That Got Us Thinking. . .

One of my firm's goals is to help Christian churches and ministries focus as much of their budget as possible on their ministry programs. Since they could save a lot of money by making their next PBX upgrade a FreePBX server, my firm needed to help them move in that direction! We started helping churches and ministries implement FreePBX phone systems because our conclusion agreed with the initial research: PBX solutions are a very mature technology, and spending tens of thousands of dollars just isn't as necessary today as it was in the late 1900s!

Options—The Biggest Challenge!

Designing a FreePBX phone system can be overwhelming because the technology is so capable, it has a lot of options. Here are some options to consider:

1. *Physical Handsets or Softphones with Headsets?*

- One option is to eliminate physical handsets (the traditional telephones that sit on the desk) and instead use softphones. Softphones are apps that run on computers, tablets, and smartphones. Some of the benefits include:

  - *More desk space for other things.* This is similar to how no longer using large CRT monitors allows for more desk space.

  - *A hands-free environment.* Softphones depend upon headsets. Most users love that!
    Headsets can be inexpensive wired units (about $30) or more expensive wireless units. Some wireless headsets are inexpensive, but my favorite one is a bit pricey (a little more than $300). Rather than using Bluetooth technology (often spotty

performance), the Sennheiser Office Runner uses radio frequency technology that gives it up to a 400-foot crystal clear range!

- ***The ability to interface with the computer or device's contact list, like Outlook.*** Using softphone apps means the softphones can interface with your contact list.

- ***Saving money.*** Buying softphones is more economical, costing less than handsets. The solution we prefer is Counterpath's Bria. Bria for Windows or Mac is about $50 (see *https://secure.counterpath.com/Store/CounterPath/*), with volume discounts available. Appropriate physical handsets—cheap ones—are at least double that; the ones my firm recommends start just under $200.

- ***Less Ethernet ports needed.*** Using softphones eliminates the need for having two Ethernet ports at each desk (optimal configuration for desks with a computer and a handset)—more on that later.

2. ***Live Attendant or Automated Attendant?*** Many churches still want a live person to answer phones rather than an automated attendant. VoIP PBXes give you multiple options, which are:

  - Live attendant;

  - Automated attendant greeting that gives options for service times and locations and a list of departments; it also encourages the caller to enter an extension if known, or to use a dial-by-name directory; or

- Live attendant backed up by an automated attendant when the live attendant isn't logged in or is unable to answer within a specified number of rings.

3. ***Hosted Off-Site or Locally On-Site?*** One of the options especially helpful for churches located in regions that experience electrical outages throughout the year is the ability to have the PBX hosted in a datacenter. Many still prefer to have it hosted locally on-site at the church, but it's nice to have the option! When hosted in a datacenter, phone communications can still happen even in a power outage by using an internet connection somewhere or running a smartphone softphone app.

VoIP phones, whether handsets or softphones, log into the PBX server. Because they are IP phones, they can log into the PBX from anywhere they have an internet connection!

This feature serves mobile workforces in the church well. For instance, if pastors like to do their sermon prep from home, they can login their handset (if they have one at home) or softphone to the PBX and it's like they are just down the hall at the church office! You can simply call them on their regular extension.

Also, when someone changes offices, they can easily keep their extension—without calling a technician to program the system!

Using the smartphone softphone app to call someone shields the cell number in the caller ID, and it instead sends the church's caller ID. This is helpful to protect church team members during off hours because it keeps everyone they call from learning their personal cell number.

One of our clients is a missions agency, and this aspect serves them *very* well. The agency's overseas office logs into the same hosted PBX as the home office, so the offices on both continents are simply extensions to each other. When team members travel overseas, they have the softphone app on their smartphone log into the PBX, and they are, again, simply an extension. They really like being able to get an outside line in the US, no matter their location. And there are no international dialing issues or long-distance rates!

Important VoIP Warnings

VoIP options may appeal to churches. They have their advantages, but they can also pose challenges. Several ways VoIP can cause problems include:

1. ***Two Ethernet ports are required.*** My firm is primarily known for data networks, and has had many clients who were previously sold a poorly set-up VoIP system. The challenge is that most churches do not have two Ethernet ports at each desk (VoIP phones connect to the church network with an Ethernet cable just as computers do). To avoid the cost of pulling more cable drops so that each workstation has at least two ports available to it, many VoIP salespeople tell folks to plug the telephone handsets into the only available Ethernet port at their desks, and then plug the computers into the phones. Some VoIP phones can pass the data through, but they usually limit the data flow the computers want and need. As primarily data people, my firm is always displeased when that happens.

This is another reason I like the softphone concept so much. It's almost like taking an algebraic equation and reversing what is on each side of the equal sign. Rather than plugging the computer into the phone, it's like plugging the phone into the computer. The phone requires very little bandwidth, so it doesn't suffer, and the computer gets all the bandwidth it needs. Win-win!

2. ***VoIP PBXes can be vulnerable to hacking.*** It is important to protect the PBX properly by putting it behind a capable firewall. Make certain you keep the PBX software and the server's OS current. Many of the patches released have security enhancements that are important to have in place.

CHURCH IT STRATEGIES

> Trying to predict the future is like
> trying to drive down a country
> road at night with no lights while
> looking out the back window.
>
> ■
>
> PETER F. DRUCKER[20]

11

IT VOLUNTEERS— YES OR NO?

> We have different gifts, according
> to the grace given to each of us.
> If your gift is . . .
>
> ■
>
> THE APOSTLE PAUL[21]

For many reasons, churches thrive when their congregations are involved in the work of the church. We love—and need—our volunteers! They are crucial to churches.

What should you do with congregants who want to volunteer to help with your IT? There are ways IT volunteers can help and there are ways they can hurt. Let's address some common issues that cause problems for church teams when volunteers are involved. The goal here is to help church IT leaders effectively use volunteers and avoid common missteps in using those volunteers.

---

[21] Romans 12:6. The Holy Bible, New International Version (1984). International Bible Society

Also, someone who volunteers for a church IT team should understand the church's perspective and priorities so that their help is most effective.

What Can Go Wrong?

When churches rely on IT volunteers, here are a few things that can go wrong:

- *Poor IT strategy.* Churches often suffer from poor IT strategies because they allow people—volunteers and staff—to learn and develop their IT skills while serving the church in this vital area. Letting people learn and grow in the church IT department sounds good, but the truth is that it is usually only good for the one learning and growing.

  When these individuals are improving their knowledge and skills, they are doing so by trial and error because that's one of the ways people learn. The unfortunate result is a less-than-optimal IT strategy and solution, leading to unnecessary break downs and wasted time for the church staff. Lost productivity is costly.

- *Fragmented IT strategy.* This is a compounding of the first point. When asked to evaluate or help with IT strategies, people bring the perspective of their experience. If that experience is different from those who came before, and it nearly always is, then any new strategy introduced will be based on the experience and perspective of the newest team member. That usually results in a fragmented IT strategy that doesn't mesh well with other strategies in place, affecting staff productivity. It will be magnified further if the perspectives invited to weigh in on the IT strategy have limited IT experience.

My firm saw this play out at a megachurch where a new congregant, who was a sales engineer for a large hardware manufacturer, introduced himself to one of the pastors after the service. When the pastor learned of the new congregant's employer, he invited him to evaluate the church's IT strategy. When the congregant did, he noted that the church experienced higher-than-normal reliability with zero downtime, but said its strategy wasn't scalable. (Scalability refers to the ability of a system to scale up to an extremely large configuration, like when a company goes global.) He recommended that the system be partially redone with scalability in mind.

The pastor agreed that scalability must be important since it is a church with global reach, so a plan and budget were created using equipment from the congregant's company. The budget was huge, and the number of church staff ten years later is about the same as it was when the sales engineer—using a term few outside of IT fully understand—sold the church on the need to be scalable. It was terrible to see so much money wasted.

• **Lack of availability.** These poor and fragmented strategy issues mean increased support needs. And volunteers generally are not available when they are needed most: when church staff are at work. Volunteers are usually only available before or after work hours. More productivity is lost because problems can't be resolved until after hours. Although the church staff usually absorbs this for a while, the dynamic often creates future conflict.

• **Burnout.** The problem comes full circle. Poor, fragmented IT strategies require more and more after-hours support from the volunteer, who eventually concludes that a choice must be made between supporting the IT strategies that he or she helped put into place or spending time with friends, family, and activities. If the volunteer pulls back or bows out, the church then must find another person to take over. And so the cycle starts again, and things will likely get worse by further IT strategy fragmentation.

Church IT Complexity

The IT needs of churches are more sophisticated in their complexity than most realize! Here's why:

- *Sophisticated complexity.* Rather than a simple list of names and contact information, churches track many dimensions of congregants' lives, including contact information, family structures, life events, interests and spiritual gifts, volunteerism, background check data for certain volunteer roles (like children's workers, for example, to ensure no pedophiles are involved), contributions, attendance, and more. In addition, churches use many audio/visual solutions (hardware and software), and they need to run with the excellence and reliability of a broadcast studio.

- *Mission critical.* Church staffs are usually smaller in number than their for-profit counterparts and have less computer application training, but they still have deadlines that must be met every week.

  Dan Bishop[22] once said the church is more like a newspaper business with daily and weekly publication deadlines than almost any other business analogy. He is

---

[22] Dan Bishop. Houston CO+OP. Houston, TX

correct! Only a reliable system can relieve the level of stress these deadlines create for smaller teams—every week, on time, every time.

- *Budget sensitivity.* Churches with small teams, working with daily and weekly deadlines, also have limited budgets. Therefore, IT strategies need to tackle sophisticated complexity and mission critical reliability as efficiently as possible. Anything less will hinder the mission of the church.

The Right Place for IT Volunteers

A few professional IT vendors specialize in helping churches meet IT needs well. At the time of this writing, I know of four or five—two of whom have a national reach. At a minimum, they can help set the overall IT strategy in your church and identify roles in which volunteers can help.

Some possible volunteer IT roles that can be successful include:

- Help desk (if they're available during work hours);

- Pulling cable;

- Moving equipment;

- Deploying/installing software (if given a step-by-step list to help achieve standardization among systems); and,

- Some periodic maintenance routines, such as cleaning keyboards, mice, and monitors/displays.

Each of these is helpful and important, and inviting

volunteers to help in these ways will be a blessing for staff members and volunteers alike.

Another way churches involve IT volunteers is to offer their communities free tech days. People in the community can bring their computers to the church to be updated, repaired, swept for viruses, and so on. What a terrific bridge-building event! In addition, it's a great way to let IT volunteers serve.

If your church hosts a free-tech day, my firm suggests that the person bringing a computer in for repair sign a release that covers such issues as:

- Liability (this is a free service);

- Inadvertent discovery of private information, such as ID numbers, credit card numbers, and so on;

- Inadvertent discovery of child porn or other illegal data with possible mandatory reporting rules that may apply.

12

TRAINING: THE MOST NEGLECTED SPEC

> Organized learning must become a
> lifelong process.
>
> ■
>
> PETER F. DRUCKER[23]

I n chapter 4, I described the best way to choose new
solutions as using a thorough analysis of needs and
an objective search (see the section titled "A Better Way,"
beginning on page 38). When using this approach, the staff
members will recognize that no solution is perfect and focus on
the 80 to 85 percent of the needs the new solution will meet.
Staff members will clean up their data, receive training, and
begin enjoying the blessings of the transition.

Then normal change and growth begin to affect the staff.
New people join the team through growth and attrition, but
the new people were not part of the software search. They never

---

[23] Drucker, P. (2006) *Classic Drucker*. Harvard Business Review

had to go through the pain of cleaning up old data and were never trained. Two things begin to happen: (1) newcomers use the software incorrectly, degrading its effectiveness; and (2) as they struggle to understand how the software works, they look for alternative solutions that are simpler for only their or their department's needs. These dynamics cause the entire staff's focus to shift from the 80 to 85 percent of the software that works to the portion that doesn't. Often, the church ends up concluding the current software doesn't work for them anymore, even though it mostly does. Lack of training is really at the heart of the problem.

Training Is the Key

Whether it is ChMS or another technological tool used, your church should prioritize ongoing training for your teams. Few IT investments will yield better returns for a church.

The two areas of IT that most affect the entire staff are ChMS and productivity tools. Here are the strategies I recommend:

- ***ChMS.*** Require on-site training by the solution provider for all staff when implementing a new system. Require on-site training every year, too.

This will:

- Give your team members the ability to discuss their "pain points," so the trainer can either show ways to improve processes or communicate those pain points to the solution provider. Caution the staff not to fall into an unwillingness to change a process because "we've always done it that way."

- Encourage your team to learn about new features the

solution offers and emphasize how these features can help fulfill your ministry vision. It's essential that the solution is continuing to grow in its abilities to meet needs, this is essential.

- Train new team members on the solution.

- Help keep the team focused on the 80 to 85 percent of met expectations rather than the 15 to 20 percent of missed expectations.

There is a cost for this strategy, but it is well worth it.

- *Productivity Software.* The best resource I've seen for training on common software like Word, Excel, Creative Suite, and so on is subscribing to *lynda.com*. It is reasonably priced (most churches create one account that all can use, though only one can use it at a time), and a terrific resource for training on many applications and skill sets. Accountability is wise, so I recommend setting up a requirement (number of sessions or specific courses) that must be completed within a specific period of time for each team member.

A Great Example

One church impressed me more than any other in regard to its software productivity and efficiency. A staff member explained to me what the church does, and I now recommend their approach often:

- *Identify your specialists.* Look for team members who have a real passion and proficiency in each of your software solutions (word processing, spreadsheets, databases, and so on). These are your specialists! Make certain you don't choose the same person for more than one or two solutions; spread the responsibility and acknowledgement around. Doing so also helps keep you from losing your entire knowledge base if one person leaves.

- *Invest in your specialists.* When you identify your specialists, tell each one they have a budget for training to get even better with their respective solution. Add the requirement of outside training to their annual review to be certain they do it. This will also help them get training material ideas for training the rest of your team!

- *Schedule regular weekly, bi-weekly, or monthly training opportunities.* Here is how to do this well:

  - Require they be attended by non-credentialed administrative staff.

  - Open them to credentialed and non-administrative staff. Advertise among the team the topic of the next session so a credentialed or non-administrative team member can attend if it is something they want to learn.

  - Rotate topics every session. For example, one week or month the topic is how to do an email mail-merge, and another week or month the topic is how to create a meaningful graphic dashboard that pulls data from the ChMS database and accounting system.

This very powerful strategy costs little and accomplishes so much! The only way it works, though, is to have the full buy-in of the senior pastor or the person responsible for staff performance and development. Otherwise, some who need it most will always be too busy to attend, which will affect all others on staff, too. In addition, it requires a champion to see it through.

In addition to raising everyone's proficiency, other benefits of this strategy are that it will:

- Encourage people identified as specialists. Most people serving in these capacities are behind-the-scenes and rarely get public recognition for the quality of the work they do in fulfilling the vision of your church.

- Relieve IT staff from needing to train team members on how to use all of the solutions at your church. The specialist may become the primary person to help others learn how to use the solutions because the entire team begins to realize questions about a specific application are more appropriate for the specialist.

- Increase the ability of your entire team to fulfill the mission of your church.

IT STAFF: INSOURCE OR OUTSOURCE?

> Only do what only you can do.
>
> ■
>
> ANDY STANLEY[24]

At one time, there might have been one computer in a church, most likely in the accounting office. The use of computers has grown dramatically since those early days of church computing. Now every staff member has at least one computer—or access to one. Computers are terrific tools that can powerfully help every team member become more productive and efficient!

With the expansion of computer use, each church will likely reach the point of realizing regular computer help is needed. That is when the church looks at bringing in a specialist.

[24] Stanley, A. (2006). *Next Generation Leader: Five Essentials for Those Who Will Shape the Future.* Sisters: Multnomah Books

But should the church "insource" by hiring the specialist as a full-time staff member? Or should the church "outsource" by hiring a firm or someone as an independent contractor? Understanding the four different IT roles in churches and how they differ (see chapter 1) is helpful when deciding whether to insource or outsource.

Most of the time outsourcing is a better strategy!

What IT Roles Are In Play?

In multisite megachurches, all four IT roles are at a level that it makes sense to hire in-house specialists. What about small- to large-sized churches (under 2,000 in average weekly worship attendance)? The answer changes to *maybe* it makes sense to hire in-house. The decision revolves around what IT disciplines are the most heavily used. Those disciplines are (see chapter 1 for more details):

• Web and graphic design;

• Audio/video;

• Social media;

• Data infrastructure.

In small- to large-sized churches, one person usually fills all of those needs, even though it is unlikely the person has the appropriate depth in all four disciplines. That's when it makes great sense to outsource some of the responsibility. Doing so allows the church to benefit from large strategies,[25] even

---

[25] By *large strategies*, I mean those IT strategies that improve system reliability, reduce overall cost, and minimize the distractions problematic systems force on staff.

though the church cannot afford to hire someone full time who possesses the levels of expertise needed to bring those large strategies in.

Acknowledging My Bias

I need to pause and acknowledge my bias here. I sensed the Lord's call to help Christian churches and ministries in this area, and established a company (MBS, Inc.) that is an outsource resource. I believe my company helps fill the data structure side of outsourcing well (and by God's grace, our clients seem to agree). So, I am a believer in the outsourcing model.

I have had the privilege of serving and consulting countless churches and ministries nationwide for nearly three decades. I have seen patterns of how churches approach this issue. Some work well. Some do not. Given that perspective, I offer a few thoughts here that may help.

Strategies that Increase IT Staff Size

My firm consulted with a large church that wanted to know if their IT Department was what it should be. They wanted us to evaluate their department efficiency, size, and quality. We conducted what we call an IT Audit to accomplish that. What we discovered was surprising, and is relevant for this chapter:

- The entire ministry staff was about 100 people. Sixteen of them were in the IT Department!

- The ministry had developed a few IT philosophies, or strategies, that drove the department to grow to such a large size:

  - Rather than buying appropriate quality enterprise-class hardware, they bought inexpensive parts and built their computers and servers to save money. The true cost to maintain that hardware, though, included a number of full-time salaries—year after year.

- The church's corporate culture included inviting the entire team to dream about what IT tools they'd like that would help them in their ministry. More than half of the IT Department were programmers to create the apps the rest of the staff asked for. The programmers also had to maintain them. Surprisingly, no one had checked to determine which were still in use!

There are strategies that can reduce the need for IT staff, and can save churches a lot of money. Here are a few:

- Buy enterprise-class hardware, and get at least a three-year warranty from the manufacturer with it. Though letting desktop and notebook warranties expire after three years makes sense, servers should always be kept under warranty. Dell, for example, will extend the warranty on a server five years! After that it should be retired or put in a non-critical role.

- Eliminate custom apps where possible. They are costly to create and to maintain.

- Outsource all but what you can't. Though we encourage you to keep help desk functionality in-house, engineering, programming, and pulling cable, etc, are good candidates for outsourcing.

When to Outsource
Though it depends on how much small- to large-sized churches

use graphics in their communications or A/V in their worship services, it seems the people most often sought for insourcing have great strengths in these disciplines. This most likely happens because—more often than not—communications and worship services are the first area with felt-needs for IT expertise. While these people may use vendors or church members to augment their skills in graphic artistry, for some reason, they are often reluctant to do so in the data structure side of IT.

The assumption is typically that the IT needs for data structure are simple: give everyone full access to whatever they want and let the staff mostly manage themselves! These systems are mostly approached with what is now called a BYOD (Bring Your Own Device) strategy.

That is okay, unless there are also servers, public WiFi, and data responsibilities to manage; if so, it makes sense to outsource. While a church may be able to get by with outsourcing as needed for web and graphic design, audio/visual, and social media needs, a much more formal approach is necessary for outsourcing data infrastructure needs.

Who Can You Trust?

In Chapter 11, I described the best approach to using volunteers in IT, which is to address the three facets of church IT needs: sophistication and complexity, mission critical dependence, and budget sensitivity (see "Church IT Complexity" beginning on page 82). With those in mind, a good outsource resource in the data infrastructure discipline should meet the following minimal criteria to serve a church well:

- *Data Infrastructure Expertise.* Because a church's IT needs are sophisticated and complex, a good IT outsource resource should have deep experience in strategizing, designing, and supporting local area networks and cloud-hosted solutions for many organizations of a size similar to your church and larger. This large perspective requires strategies that minimize downtime and support needs. If your team needs to use your church's systems without distraction, this is important.

- ***Church IT Expertise.*** Because a church's IT needs are mission critical and budget sensitive, a good outsource resource should have the experience of working with many churches and ministries. Otherwise, it is likely the firm will not understand the mission critical nature of how church teams rely on their systems to fulfill their calling, while also meeting the constant flow of weekly deadlines. The natural inclination will be to utilize costly over-spec'd systems sold by the resource (which would waste funds) or consumer-class systems that cannot meet the reliability needs of the staff. Neither is a good use of funds, and those with church IT expertise know that.

- ***Church Software Expertise.*** Just like hospitals use software unique to their needs, as do accounting, legal, and engineering firms, churches use unique software to meet their needs. Whether it's your ChMS database, a non-profit accounting package, presentation software, or event scheduling and registration software, the outsource resource needs to know how those systems work and what they require. Some have very specific and unique requirements, and delivering reliability means knowing how to configure the systems so the underlying infrastructure is supportive to them.

One of the key considerations when looking for an IT vendor is to look for one with multiple staff. My firm recently spoke with a church whose IT vendor died. He was a one-person shop. The church felt he served well, but he had not documented the church's system. When he died, it was up to the church or the church's next IT vendor to figure out how the system was configured.

I mentioned that my firm is an outsource resource, but it's important to note that there are a few other firms who also focus on serving churches nationwide well. Here is a list of the four in alphabetical order (my firm included, of course!):

- Acts Group (*actsgroup.net*)

- BEMA (*bemaservices.com*)

- MBS, Inc. (*mbsinc.com*)

- Solerant (*solerant.com*)

Contacting any of these four can help move your church forward in developing a solid IT data infrastructure strategy and deliver the expertise you need.

14

WHO OWNS YOUR PUBLIC DNS RECORD?

> *Dovorey no provorey.*
> That means trust but verify.
>
> ■
>
> RONALD REAGAN[26]

DNS stands for Domain Name System, the worldwide method to help people find things on the internet. For instance, opening a browser and typing in the address field *mbsinc.com* will take you to my firm's website.

DNS is how the internet knows where our website is. It stores the IP address for each website and more.

DNS runs on innumerable servers around the world, so that regardless of where your website is hosted, someone anywhere in the world can connect to it.

Your church's public DNS record is the record that the internet uses to point others to your websites, your email

---

[26] Reagan, R. (1986, October 23) Remarks at a Senate Campaign Rally for Christopher S. Bond in Springfield, MO

server, and potentially much more. So, who owns your public DNS record and why does it matter?

Why Is DNS Record Ownership Important?

One way to think of DNS is to think of your street address or home phone number. Both are important in how people in your community reach you, and an interruption would mean that people would not easily find you. In today's culture, if an attempt to find you takes too long or fails, an individual will likely lose interest and move on.

That is exactly what happens when someone tries to get to your website or send you an email. With even a minimal delay, let alone a problem, people will simply move on.

Public DNS Record Access

Technology is constantly changing. When you change or add IT services (like email or instant messaging), change internet service providers, change server configurations, and so on, doing so often requires making a change to your public DNS record. More likely than not, there will come a time when someone working with your website or email system will want to make a change to your public DNS record. We often encounter this as we begin working with new clients. Many times, no one at the church knows how to access and modify the DNS record. The cost common reasons why are:

- A volunteer or staff member created the church's first website or email server, and set up a DNS record accordingly. At the time, it was done under this person's name with his or her credentials (user ID and password), and he or she never thought to properly document it or transfer it into the church's name.

- When the church set up its first website or email server, the web host set up the DNS for it.

Both situations need to be addressed, and here is why:

- In the case of DNS record ownership by a volunteer or staff member, what happens when the relationship with that person and your church ends? For various reasons, volunteers sometimes change churches, as do team members. In either case, if DNS ownership moves with them, making future changes will be more difficult than it should be. It could be even more difficult if the person has died, and the record ownership is in probate or with heirs who are not friendly to your church.

- All businesses—churches included—need the freedom to change vendors at any time and for any reason. If a web host holds ownership to the church's DNS record, making a change in that relationship can be problematic. An employee of the web host could try to use the DNS record as a bargaining chip to keep the church there.

What Is the Best Approach?

My firm's new clients often ask us if we want to take on their DNS record ownership. Our answer is always no. We need access to it to do our work, but the church should maintain ownership of its DNS record.

We usually recommend the church move its DNS record to DNSMadeEasy.[27] Their annual fee is reasonable, and this keeps the DNS record in a neutral environment. Then, the church

---

[27] www.dnsmadeeasy.com

can grant access to whomever it wants as needed, or revoke that access as needed.

If you don't know who owns your church's DNS record, this should be a high priority. Find out where it is, who has access to it, and take ownership of it.

15

DISASTER RECOVERY AND BUSINESS CONTINUITY

Be prepared.

■

BOY SCOUTS MOTTO[28]

I t's unfortunate that disasters of all types happen and they can happen at any time. That's why there's a robust news reporting industry—every day there are new disasters to talk about! Some are natural, some are manmade, but they all have the same impact of disrupting lives.

September 11, 2001, changed many things in the US. More lives were lost in the three attacks that day than were lost in the Pearl Harbor attack on December 7, 1941.[29] No one knows how many businesses were also killed that day, but it's safe to say

---

[28] Boy Scouts of America. *www.scouting.org/About/FactSheets/OverviewofBSA.aspx*, accessed 8/12/2015

[29] National Commission on Terrorist Attacks Upon the United States, The 9/11 Commission Report Executive Summary

that the number was large because the data necessary to sustain their operations (accounts receivable, accounts payable, various documents and spreadsheets, databases, and so on) was not properly backed up.

The same is true of major *natural* disasters, such as hurricanes, tsunamis, tornados, earthquakes, and fires. This is a picture of a church that was severely impacted by Hurricane Katrina.[30]

Many appropriately consider disaster recovery to be one of IT's highest priorities.

Backup Strategies

The goal of any good backup strategy is to protect data from threats that could destroy it. There are many backup strategies. The best backup strategies are automatic, comprehensive, tested, and include an off-site storage component. Here are details on all of those:

- *Automatic.* Manually triggered backups are guaranteed to fail. Backups aren't needed very often, and any computer user can easily fall into the *I don't have time today* syndrome, which then develops into a backup system that is never run. Backups should run regularly, automatically, and unattended.

---

[30] First Baptist Church in Gulfport, MS (2005). Photo by Greg Warner, used with permission.

- **Comprehensive.** I am not a fan of partial backups, also known as incremental backups. The problem is that when restoring data, time is usually tight. The longer it takes to find all the needed files and restore them, the more stressful the situation will be. A comprehensive backup avoids that stress.

- **Tested.** There's nothing worse than running your first backup test while trying to recover from a disaster, and *then* learning that the backups weren't doing what you hoped.

I learned this the hard way when my team and I were helping a client replace the Network Operating System (NOS) of a server. Our first step was to run a comprehensive backup and have the backup software confirm that the backup was good by comparing file names, dates, and sizes. Once that was done, we deleted the server's partitions (effectively erasing any possible data on the hard drives), then we installed the new NOS, installed the backup software, and then restored the backup we had just created. We were shocked to learn that the backup, though it passed the compare test, was worthless! All of the characters in the files were null characters (null characters look like this: ☐)! Using some tech tools, we restored most of the data, but it made for a long and embarrassing night.

- **Include an off-site component.** A copy of a recent backup needs to be taken off-site in case there's a disaster large enough to take out the server room. The September 11 attacks on the Twin Towers and the flooding from Hurricane Katrina damaged or destroyed many on-site server rooms.
The off-site backup must be comprehensive. It cannot be

an incremental backup. Some prefer online backups such as Carbonite or CrashPlan to accomplish this. More about that shortly.

Backups come in many flavors and strategies. Differences between backups include incremental vs. comprehensive, system level *vs.* file-level, server-only vs. server plus computers *vs.* computers-only, and more. The server component is further complicated if your servers are virtual machines running on a host using a hypervisor like VMware or HyperV.

What I Recommend and Why

Networks and computers store data. Some data is mission-critical, but not all of it. Even still, a loss of any and all data would take a lot of time to re-create and would slow down productivity while doing so.

I recommend backing up the entire system. The objection sometimes voiced is that doing so would require a lot of capacity. Appropriate capacity is reasonably inexpensive, and it needs to be seen in a similar light as an insurance policy.

For networks with servers and computers, I recommend the following:

- Configure all computers so they save their data to the server by default. It will save time and money not having to back up each computer on the network.

- Back up servers that store data every night. Do not run incremental backups—only run full backups. If the servers are virtual, use a backup solution, such as Veeam, that backs up the servers so they can be quickly restored in their entirety if necessary.

- Back up to tape drives. A good strategy is to have at least 20 tapes (four weeks' worth), and to rotate them daily. Label them as Week 1—Monday, Week 1—Tuesday, and so on through Friday; Week 2—Monday, Week 2—Tuesday, and so on through Friday; and Week 3 and Week 4 similarly. This will be helpful if someone discovers that an important file is corrupt, and the last time they had a good copy was three weeks ago, for example.

  Larger churches might choose to back up to an enterprise-class Network Attached Storage (NAS) or Storage Area Network (SAN) device. Those who don't have those devices should avoid backing up to external portable hard drives. External portable hard drives have many moving parts and are susceptible to breakage, which would render the backup on that device unusable without an expensive restoration process that will take more than a week *may* work.

  Backing up to tape is still corporate America's preference.

- Take one tape off-site each week, rotating it with the tape from the previous week. If, like most churches, your biggest data processing day of the week is Monday or Tuesday, the backup made the night of your biggest data processing day is the one that should be rotated off-site each week. That way you can always get back to within a week of your data if a large catastrophe impacts your church.

  If you're a large church and backing up to an enterprise-class NAS or SAN, you will want to setup a second NAS or SAN off-site with data replication (an automated process in which one of these devices automatically replicates its data over a cable or internet connection) to accomplish the geographic separation component of your backup strategy.

To save money, some churches 'partner' with another church in which they replicate to each other's sites.

• Test your backups on at least a monthly basis. Keep an accountability spreadsheet to identify the backup data that was tested, the date it was tested, and what portion of the data structure was tested. The spreadsheet will help ensure that different sections of the data are tested and that, in fact, the testing happens.

What about Online Backups?

Online backup solutions are good for consumers' computers but not necessarily good for servers. The amount of data that would need to be restored on a server is usually so large that it could take weeks to download it all from an online service. Online services offer to send a copy on a hard drive if needed quickly, but the organizations I know that tried this approach were not pleased with the results.

Online backups are usually good for consumers who want to back up their data files, such as photos. Some clients of ours still use an online backup service to automate the off-site requirement and only use them to restore single files; they also have an on-site backup in case of a more severe disaster.

Setting an Appropriate Backup Budget

All technology costs something and thus requires a budget. Many in IT assume all data needs to be quickly restorable at all times. That strategy, however, may be too costly and beyond the reach of most churches.

The best way to set the backup strategy and budget is to ask church leadership to prioritize various categories of data and assign a maximum time frame within which data must be restored following a disaster. In addition to helping set an appropriate backup system budget, this will help leadership think in terms of business continuity. (Business Continuity Plans detail how to continue operations in and following a major disaster.)

Typical categories of data include audio and video files, databases, email, and productivity documents like word processing files, spreadsheets, and so on. You may even want to break those categories down further to help leadership with this task. For instance, word processing files might include letters, bulletins, policies and procedures, and so on.

Often, leadership will assign the highest priority to communication systems and databases—email, financial databases, and non-financial databases. An example would be that email, telephones, and ChMS databases need to be restored within two hours, and everything else within three days.

After leadership assigns time frames for data restoration, design a backup strategy to meet the requirements and present it for approval. If leaders think the budget is too high, ask them to adjust some of the time frames they assigned to the data categories so you can redesign the strategy accordingly.

Business continuity is leadership's responsibility and disaster recovery is IT's responsibility. The only way a backup strategy budget can be appropriately set is with leadership's guidance.

How I Back Up Data

My firm hosts servers for many Christian churches and ministries in a high-end datacenter. We use Veeam to back up those servers, which gives us the ability to restore individual files or complete servers quickly. Our servers are also in our datacenter, so our data is protected.

The way we host file servers is unique, and is a helpful

illustration for this chapter. We put all of our clients' data files in a file server that is all theirs—not shared with any other clients. We use a solution called Owncloud to provide access to data files. It works very much like Dropbox, but it has better security, and the data is private (though sharable). The data synchronizes to team members' hard drives (just like Dropbox), so it is almost as if they have second copies through that method.

I use a MacBook that has a very large hard drive. On my Mac, I have Owncloud replicate our firm's entire data structure (not our clients' data, just ours). Granted, that takes Owncloud a little longer to synchronize, but there is a terrific benefit. The Mac OS includes a great app called Time Machine, which backs up my entire hard drive to an external drive whenever I am working at my desk. I use an external backup drive that is big enough to maintain more than a year's worth of Time Machine backups. In addition to the other protections my firm has in place, I can also quickly access all of our data with file versioning going back more than a year to find that last uncorrupted version of a file when needed!

Redundancy of backup layers is helpful. When I can find a file that was discovered to be corrupt or missing, team members see me as heroic! At times like that, the little extra spent to have that extra layer of protection is never thought of as an over expend.

16

THE SECURITY SWEETSPOT

> Find the 'sweet spot' between absolute transparency and non-transparency—it's called appropriate transparency—where trust is maximized with minimal disruption or risk to the ministry.
>
> ■
>
> DAN BUSBY[31]

Chapter 2 explained the importance of team members being thought of as customers of the church's IT Department. The chapter also described some of the ramifications of that approach to managing technology in churches. One topic in that chapter was giving *local admin* status to all team members (see "Here's a Practical Example," beginning on page 24), which some argue is a weakening of the church's system security. On page 25, I mention two ways to overcome those security concerns.

[31] Busby, D. (2015). Trust. Winchester, VA: ECFAPress

Additional customer satisfaction issues for team members include our firm's approach to password strategies, off-site file access, and WiFi access. How one approaches security affects each of these.

Security Is Important!

Strong system security is critical. Much of the data we have in churches is sensitive: the most common are counseling notes, board minutes, HR documentation, contributions information, and database records. Churches need to do their due diligence to protect all of it.

Many people today question anything less than a full-access approach to church data. However, some of the data that churches have can harm people or the church if let into the wild. Consider these scenarios:

- In some states, like California, where I live, there is a state constitutional right to privacy. If I were a terminated church employee and my termination details or contact information was not properly safeguarded by the church, and I felt somehow harmed by that lack of protection, I could sue for a violation of my right to privacy.

- A church board is working through a sticky issue, such as the possible church discipline of a member as detailed in Matthew 18, and has referenced its discussion in its minutes. That is sensitive information that could hurt the individual and the church if it were not adequately protected.

- A church's vendor sensed the value of the church's database and exported a copy of it. The vendor then began renting it as a list in the community. Consider the contents of that database and the possible damage it could do! The database included contact information, children's names, tithing records, life events, Social Security Numbers of employees, and more.

A church's data must be protected with firewalls and passwords.

Password Strategies

Many churches have annual audits performed by CPA firms, often to satisfy the terms of building loans or to help demonstrate integrity in their finances to a watching world. Both are good reasons, and CPA audits are very helpful in many ways. The Sarbanes-Oxley Act of 2002 was enacted in response to accounting scandals in some very large companies. One of its many effects is that CPA auditors now ask about many IT issues. This is part of their due diligence to see if things are being done correctly. Many of those auditors do not have professional IT training or experience, and simply work through a series of questions and record responses.

Through this process CPAs have heightened everyone's sense of appropriate IT security. Some things they brought attention to are very good, such as locked server rooms. However, on password strategies, they may have hurt us by recommending we change passwords every ninety days. The practice of changing passwords so often in churches actually *lowers* security! Church team members are like most computer users. When they change their passwords, they often write them on Post-It® notes or tape them to their monitors and displays.

In a March 2, 2016 post on the U.S. FCC's website[32], policies requiring regular password changes was said to be

---

"less beneficial than previously thought, and sometimes even counterproductive"! They go on in that post to reference two studies that caused them to draw the conclusion that "frequent mandatory [password] expiration inconveniences and annoys users without as much security benefit as previously thought, and may even cause some users to behave less securely."

I have been saying that for years!

What my firm recommends instead is the following password policy:

- Passwords must be a minimum of seven characters and include uppercase and lowercase alpha characters, numbers, and common punctuation. This is a great minimum in that it accommodates most Bible references!

- Passwords must never be shared with others, and they never expire. They will be replaced if a breach occurs.

- Passwords can only be set by the IT Department and are maintained in an encrypted file for reference.

This policy makes for easy-to-remember passwords since it accommodates verse references. This helps to eliminate the Post-It® note issue. If people tell IT they need a new password because they shared it with someone, IT can give them a new one and update their documentation. If someone does that often, the situation should be referred to leadership for possible action.

Firewalls

A firewall is a solution that keeps unwanted outsiders from accessing your computer systems. We need to guard against internet bots and people—the two major threats from the outside. Here's more details on both:

- Internet bots are little apps that roam the internet looking
  for exploitable ports into networks and computers. They
  are incessant, and their technology is constantly morphing
  into new threats. For that reason, it is essential that firewalls
  receive constant updates to help them identify new technology
  threats. Many firewall companies offer an annual subscription
  to meet this need.

- People who want to gain access into networks and computers
  include former employees, family members, and others in the
  community. Some have no malicious intent, but some do. The
  fact that some have bad intentions is why it is essential to have
  a policy of never sharing passwords.

Firewalls, aided by good password strategies, help protect
churches from these threats.

There are software firewalls and hardware firewalls. Either
can be good, depending on their spec. My firm's favorite spec is
the Dell SonicWALL firewall series. SonicWALLs provide the
features that most churches need at a reasonable cost while not
overcharging them for many features they will likely never use.

One of SonicWALL's features that my firm likes is that it
can also filter internet content; this prevents people using the
church's WiFi from getting to websites the church considers
inappropriate.

A good firewall and a good password policy help protect
data from those within the church who shouldn't have access
to certain sensitive data and from those outside the church.
Firewalls and password policies can enforce access rules that
augment the network security systems in place.

Off-Site Access

System users today are very mobile. Some study and prep off-site, some need access to congregant data from off-site, and more. There's more than one way to provide secure access from off-site. Here are a few of the most prevalent:

- *VPN Access.* This is probably the highest level of security for off-site access used by churches. A VPN is a *Virtual Private Network* even though it connects over the internet. A VPN accomplishes a higher level of security by creating an encrypted link, and requires the off-site system to run an app that has the digital key to unencrypt the link. It has some strengths and weaknesses:

  - *Strength:* VPNs provides the highest level of simple security for off-site access.

  - *Weakness:* VPNs require the off-site user to run an app to establish the VPN link, which is often more than what most in ministry can successfully deal with technologically. It's not that the app is difficult to run; it's that it requires an extra step to gain access that is often forgotten and generates frustration and support requests. VPNs are not intuitive.

- *Hosted databases.* Many ChMS databases are now hosted and available via browser (like Firefox, Safari, Edge, and so on). This automates the security when they are hosted on secure servers (an important requirement for a hosted ChMS). It has some strengths and weaknesses:

  - *Strength:* Data security access is automated, making it

easily available to off-site staff and volunteers.

- **Weakness:** The only data available is what is in the database. If there is additional data, like spreadsheets or documents, for example, they may not be available in this manner.

• **Remote Desktop Connection.** Data is available on a server that requires a connection, but the connection may not be highly secure. It looks like accessing data on a typical Windows server.

- **Strength:** The interface is familiar and more intuitive than the process of establishing a VPN, and it looks like typical data access on a Windows server.

- **Weakness:** Remote desktop sessions can be susceptible to what is called a *Man in the Middle Attack*, in which someone monitoring internet traffic might intercept data being transferred. Some IT people add a security certificate and secure the connection to help strengthen the security of this method.

• **Remote Data Synchronization.** Many use an app, like Dropbox or Owncloud, to synchronize data between devices. The net effect is that data can be stored on the mobile device *and* on the server, with changes made to it synchronized in real time if both are connected via network or internet connection.

- **Strength:** This method, once it's configured, is fully automatic and requires no user intervention. On devices with storage capacity, like notebook computers, data can be stored locally on the mobile device and accessed as needed with or without an internet connection; changes will be synchronized automatically if or when connected.

- *Weakness:* Data on mobile devices increases risk if those devices are not adequately protected by their user, getting lost or stolen. Thus, security training is recommended. Also, some of these apps do not have good security, so if they require storing data on a public cloud server, they may not be a good solution. Dropbox is one whose security is questionable, which is why I prefer Owncloud (private cloud server with more tightly controlled access).

Mobile Device Vulnerability

By their very nature, mobile devices (smartphones, tablets, and notebook computers) are more vulnerable than other devices. They are more easily stolen or lost, so a strategy should be in place to delete any sensitive data from a stolen device. Some data synchronization services help, as do some mobile device operating systems. The strategy to delete sensitive data should be driven by the operating system and apps on the mobile device.

Churches should also have a defined process to delete sensitive data from terminated employees' mobile devices.

17

THE VALUE OF STANDARDIZATION

> Manage for results.
>
> ■
>
> JOHN PEARSON[33]

When I was earning my business administration degree (with a focus on management), I formed a philosophy that shaped the way I approach the use of computers: *Good managers get the best possible results from limited resources.*

Good Management

As a Christian, I want to hear at the end of my earthly journey, "Well done, good and faithful servant. ... Come and share your master's happiness!"[34] My guess is that you feel the same way! So, how does a faithful servant, or in today's vernacular, a *good manager*, earn such praise?

---

[33] Pearson, J. (2008). *Mastering the Management Buckets*. Ventura, CA: Regal

[34] Matthew 25:21. The Holy Bible, New International Version (1984). International Bible Society

The first important lesson is one taught by Jesus himself. He was a servant leader. The Last Supper is a great example—Jesus lowered himself to wash the feet of his friends. Then, he even served the one he knew would betray him! Serving with love and humility is essential.

In every job, managers wrestle with limited resources. Whether it is restricted cash flows, teams that are too small for the task, equipment that is less than optimal, or something else, there is always at least one challenge. Yet, there is a job to do and goals to accomplish. Good managers, like race car drivers, do their best to keep RPMs and speeds as high as possible without blowing up the engine.

Similarly, a servant leader does his or her best to keep the team motivated and moving forward. Because servant leaders have an underlying posture of love and humility, they don't push their teams beyond what can be endured. They ensure team members are paid enough to care for themselves and their families, have enough downtime to get refreshed, and have appropriate tools available to help them with as few distractions as possible. That last point is where standardization has its impact.

Standardization

As my team and I began deploying larger and larger networks, we developed standards that helped us configure workstations. These standards helped us create workstations that fulfilled our clients' needs to accomplish their ministry goals without distractions. Over time, we found that some computer configuration settings helped and some hindered.

As we began to identify optimal configurations, we found it challenging to deliver those consistently on every workstation. It was easy to miss a setting or two on any given computer, and our lack of consistency caused support tickets. We saw the value in achieving standardization and needed a way to deliver it.

We developed a checklist system for each computer configuration: servers, Windows, Macs, and for each Operating System. Having a method of delivering a standardized configuration, we noticed that:

- Client satisfaction continued to increase, keeping pace as we began working for larger churches and ministries.

- *Support tickets* remained low despite the larger number of systems we were supporting.

Focusing on high-quality standardization helps keep our clients' support costs low. As we think of their call to build the Kingdom, that translates into fewer distractions and higher results. It means we're helping them achieve the best possible results with limited resources!

MBS' Setup Checklist
Here are some excerpts from our checklists for Windows 10 and Mac OSX that you may find to be a helpful start:

- Windows 10

  - Windows Explorer Configuration & Actions

    - ❑ At the Root of the C drive, go to the View tab

    - ❑ Set List to View (this is a better view for most users)

    - ❑ Check File Name Extensions (most users want to see

file extensions, and it helps with support)

- Control Panel Settings & Configuration

  - ❏ Sound: click the Sounds tab, then click Sound Scheme, then click No Sounds (helps to minimize office distractions)

  - ❏ Sound: while on the Sounds tab, uncheck Play Windows Startup Sounds (helps to minimize office distractions)

  - ❏ Display: Adjust Resolution and/or Text Size

  - ❏ Screen Saver: set to none (helps reduce support issues)

- Mac OSX

  - Finder Preferences

    - ❏ On the General tab, set New Finder windows to open to the user's home folder (speeds up finding files)

    - ❏ On the Sidebar Favorites tab, remove all checks except desktop and home folder (speeds up finding files and is less confusing)

    - ❏ With the Finder window open, click the View menu option (at top of the screen). Check Show as Columns, Show Path Bar, and Show Status Bar (columns is a better view for most users, and the Path Bar and Status Bar are very helpful in folder navigation and support)

- Safari Preferences

  ❏ Set downloads to automatically go to the Desktop (helps the user remember to delete downloads that are no longer needed, saving storage space)

  ❏ Set the church's standard home page

We also include a section detailing which apps should be installed on every system (like Firefox, Microsoft Office, Thirtyseven4 for anti-malware, and so on).

This type of standardization helps users be more efficient, and it helps the support team when it responds to users requests. The users can change whatever they want, of course, but at least they each have a common starting point and are more predictable as a result.

The mistake most people make is not standardizing, which means every machine is different based on how it was setup by the manufacturer and may not be properly set up to run well for the user. Non-standardized systems tend to be more confusing to users and more challenging to support.

18

CHANGING PARADIGMS: THE CLOUD & BYOD

> The price of doing the same old thing is far higher than the price of change.
>
> ■
>
> BILL CLINTON[35]

At the time of this writing, it is just nine years after Apple introduced the iPhone and eight years after Google introduced the Android. While there were smartphone-like devices (the Palm Treo, for example) in the past, it wasn't until the iPhone that smartphones became mainstream. Those devices definitely changed the way we think about using technology today.

---

[35] Clinton, W. (1994). Public Papers of the Presidents of the United States, William J. Clinton, 1993 Book I: January 20 to July 31, 1993. US Government Printing Office

Churches occasionally ask me to help map out a ten-year IT strategy. In response, I point to recent technological changes, including smartphones and tablets, as examples of how fast things change. These churches then understand that ten years is too far out to plan! I suggest a two-year plan (the plan is a list of things they need to accomplish), which is based on a three- to five-year horizon (identifying the general direction where they want their ministry to go, sort of like a compass heading).

Two major paradigm changes are wildly affecting the planning for IT strategies and structures: The Cloud and the "Bring Your Own Device" (BYOD) movement.

The Cloud

The cloud is a paradigm shift that is already mature, and many churches have begun taking advantage of its benefits.

Most of us, when we think of the cloud, think of social media platforms, email solutions, and online databases or backups. Those are important and make a difference. But the greater potential impact of the cloud is more than those services, and that impact really helps churches the most.

For decades, my firm has installed and configured local area networks (LANs) for churches nationwide. Those LANs require major capital investments in hardware, software, and engineering, which significantly impacts cash flow. The cloud can remove that large capital expense. This is the cloud's greatest potential for churches because it allows them to focus more of their cash flow toward ministry programming.

How much capital expense does it remove? Compare the costs of these two real situations (circa 2015) for a large, single-site church (with about 2,000 in average weekly attendance). The ChMS provider already hosts their ChMS:

Item	Locally-Based	Cloud-Based
Hardware	two servers (one as a host for multiple virtual servers and one as a bare metal server to host backup and a few other services), two UPSes (uninterruptable power supplies), a backup drive, and twenty tapes—$12,830	none
Software	VMware vSphere Essentials (hypervisor for the new host), Windows 2012 r2 for up to ten total servers (running on the host and the backup server) with client access licenses (CALs), Exchange 2013 server with fifty mailbox licenses, Veeam backup software—$3,415	Exchange licenses—$315
Engineering	$30,970	$6,720
Total Start	$47,215	$7,035
Monthly Hosting Fee	none	$850

The immediate project savings is more than $40,000! The monthly hosting fee would not catch up to that savings for four years! By then, the church would have started planning its next major network upgrade.

The cloud provides churches with a major savings. It allows funds that would have been spent on hardware, software, and engineering to instead be invested elsewhere in ministry.

The key with cloud-hosted services is to keep your church's data private, safe, and secure. That requires some due diligence when selecting cloud-hosting vendor(s).

Chapter 13 explained how to select an outsource vendor (see "Who Can You Trust?" beginning on page 95), and in addition to that, add the following two criteria:

- **Private vs. Public Cloud.** There are two halves to the cloud: *Public Cloud* and *Private Cloud*. Public cloud vendors allow anyone to create an account begin using their services. This includes Facebook, Twitter, Dropbox, and so on. Private cloud vendors require users to have been pre-approved for access to connect to servers and services; they are not open and available to anyone.

  Understanding this difference is important because churches have a lot of sensitive data. With increasing threats toward sensitive data, safeguards are essential. Placing sensitive data only in a private cloud vendor's servers is an appropriate safeguard

- **Datacenter Rating.** Datacenters are rated on their infrastructure redundancies: the higher the redundancies of power, internet trunks, and ability to manage HVAC, the greater the likelihood of uptime (staying up and running). Below is a quick explanation of the ratings[36] (lower number ratings are not as good as higher ratings):

Tier Rating	Redundancy	% Uptime	Max Hours Downtime
1	no redundancy (only one source of power, only one internet trunk, only one way to manage HVAC)	99.671%	up to 22.8 hours of downtime annually
2	partial redundancy	99.749%	up to 22 hours of downtime annually
3	full redundancy, a.k.a. N+1 fault tolerance	99.982%	up to 1.6 hours of downtime annually

---

[36] Colocation America. *http://www.colocationamerica.com/*, accessed 8/21/2015

Tier Rating	Redundancy	% Uptime	Max Hours Downtime
4	at least double redundancy, a.k.a. 2N+1 fault tolerance	99.995%	up to 26.3 minutes of downtime annually

I recommend a minimum datacenter certification of Tier 3, and prefer Tier 4. Those tiers ensure the highest level of data availability.

BYOD

BYOD is another paradigm shift gaining momentum. A BYOD situation is one in which a church team member uses his or her device instead of the one supplied by the church. A small number of churches have begun taking advantage of its benefits so far, and that number is growing.

I am not sure why folks would prefer to use their own devices unless they would rather work in a different operating system (Windows or Mac) than the one on the device supplied by the church. However, my firm even gets requests from individuals whose devices run the same OS as that of the church-supplied device!

This trend will likely continue and grow. The cloud's ubiquitous access to data and apps makes it a viable option.

BYOD makes most IT professionals uncomfortable. Historically, we have been able to keep devices not owned and configured by us off our networks. As IT people, we are responsible for protecting the data, so this has been the right thing to do. This policy has allowed us to protect data from malware and other threats. BYOD increases threats to the data if the BYOD strategy is not implemented carefully.

I wrote an article in late 2013 called "Reasonable & Essential BYOD Policies,"[37] because of this trend. While researching for that article I was surprised to learn the only BYOD policies in place in corporate America at that time dealt with smartphones! My conclusion was that churches were leading this trend, perhaps because it's more acceptable to ask in a church setting, whereas maybe it's not okay to ask in corporate America (at least, not yet). Anyway, BYOD arrangements can work for churches—and save those churches money. I recommend a minimum set of policies to protect the church and team members with BYOD arrangements.

In a recent Church IT Network online discussion, Jonathan Puddle (Director of Retail, Publishing, and Technology for the Catch the Fire ministry and a volunteer at his church) said his church is almost entirely BYOD! "We don't buy people machines anymore. We give them a cash rebate instead. … We mitigated against the cost of upgrades by pushing the whole thing to the users. Our staff buy their own personal machines and we provide a rebate. It has saved us tons. We did have to relax our management on the machines to accomplish this, but the end result has been great." The move saved the church a lot of money and increased its team members' satisfaction! What a great way to help achieve what Clif Guy said (see page 24) about trying to have a default "yes" posture!

BYOD is a growing technology trend, and churches are leading the way! Some implementation methods I am seeing churches use are:

- *SYOM, Spend Your Own Money.* This is the example mentioned above by Puddle. His church gives a rebate based

---

[37] Article available via MBS' website at *http://www.mbsinc.com/reasonable-essential-byod-policies/*

on a formula that considers the team member's role on the church staff and a percentage of the purchase cost with a cap.

- *CYOM, Choose Your Own Machine.* Based on team members' roles on the church staff, they get a budget that can be applied to a list of pre-approved computer choices. If the system they select is beyond the established budget for that role, their department can choose to cover the additional cost out of its budget.

To make these types of arrangements work, the data needs better protection than it otherwise would need because of the increased threats that BYOD introduces. That protection should include better firewalls (don't just rely on the internet service provider's router settings) and malware protection (like Thirtyseven4), as well as a better disaster recovery plan (a good backup strategy)—including more depth of backup history (I recommend a minimum of one month's backups for all churches; more when BYOD is in play).

BYOD Policies

Since BYOD requests are on the rise, it's wise for churches to research this subject now and form policies *before* a team member asks to use his or her own device. Here is a starter list of what should be covered in a policy:

Team Member Responsibilities

- *To be productive.* Team members who request to use their personal computers and/or devices must understand that they are responsible to be productive. Thus any such BYOD request, if granted, will require that they be at least as productive as they would have been using the systems normally provided by the church. Setting the standards of productivity is the responsibility of management, and team members who are not as productive on their personally-owned computers and/or devices will be required to use church-provided systems.

- *To be cooperative.* Personally-owned computers and/or devices, if allowed to be used at work, must meet minimum standards. Those standards will be set and modified from time to time by the IT Department and may address minimum processor chipsets and operating system versions, amount of RAM and storage, and the use of specific church-provided applications such as productivity suites (like Microsoft Office), anti-malware tools (like Thirtyseven4), email clients, and more. Use of substitute applications must be approved by both the IT Department and the team member's direct supervisor.

- *To be responsible.* The team member agrees to maintain their personally-owned computers and/or devices that have been approved for use at work at a level that meets or exceeds (1) productivity levels set by management and (2) the IT Department's minimum system requirements. The team member is responsible for any costs due to failed hardware, configuration and/or software issues, and theft or breakage.

- *To protect.* Team team member agrees to maintain the security of their personally-owned computers and/or devices to protect the data and integrity of the church's systems; to let their supervisor and the IT Department know if their device has been lost or stolen; and to let the church install software that could delete the church's data if the church so desires, with or without notice. The team member agrees to submit their personally-owned computers and/or devices approved for use at work for inspection by the IT Department to confirm that the system is being properly protected against malware and other threats. The team member acknowledges that the church might see data and files that could otherwise be considered private, but agrees to hold the church harmless against any claims against loss of privacy in exchange for the church agreeing to allow the team member to use his or her personally-owned computers and/or devices for work.

Church Responsibilities

- *To provide a productive environment.* The church agrees to provide a suitable work area to help the team member be productive at levels required by management. In case the team member's personally-owned computers and/or devices are not available due to required repairs (for which the team member is responsible), the church will provide a substitute computer or device using church-owned computers and/or devices for a reasonable period of time.

- *To be reasonably accommodating.* When a team member requests permission to use their personally owned computer or device at work, the church agrees to be reasonably accommodating if the team member can demonstrate that their productivity will meet or exceed the productivity standards set by the church.

- *To be supportive.* The church is not responsible to support the team member's computer or device. However, the church will give help desk support at the same level as it does for church-owned computers on the use of software provided by the church.

- *To explain Exempt vs Non-Exempt issues.* Some team members are subject to overtime rules based on state and/or federal law. The church is responsible to explain the team member's exempt or non-exempt status, and how that impacts work time recordkeeping.

Termination Procedures
If a team member is terminated by the church or initiates termination of the employment relationship, the team member agrees to remove all church-owned software and data from their personally-owned computer or device, or to provide it to the IT Department to allow the IT Department to remove the church-owned software and data.

Signed Acknowledgement
The team member and his or her supervisor will sign an agreement acknowledging the BYOD policies in place. The acknowledgement will also state that the church may modify the BYOD policy at any time and without prior notice.

GLOSSARY OF TERMS

A

Apps. The applications used on computers to accomplish tasks, also referred to as software.

Auto Attendant. An internal telephone system's receptionist or operator that is *not* a live person, but instead is a recorded voice offering a set of menu options to the caller.

B

Backup. The practice of making copies of data as part of a disaster recovery plan.

BCP, Business Continuity Plan. A detailed plan of how an organization will continue operations during a disaster.

BYOD, Bring Your Own Device. Allowing organization team members to use their own computers rather than requiring them to only use those provided by the organization.

C

ChMS, Church Management Software. Database systems that help churches track congregants' contact information, contributions, attendance, and volunteer involvement. Some ChMS solutions also provide an accounting solution unique to the accounting needs of churches.

CYOM, Choose Your Own Machine. Allowing organization team members to choose their computers from a menu of options rather than requiring them to use a specific configuration.

Church IT Network. The Church IT Network, a.k.a. CITRT, is a group of church-specific IT people who gather to help each other with proven solutions and encourage each other through the challenges of managing IT in churches.

The Cloud. There are many ways to define the cloud. The easiest definition is that the data and apps are stored and accessed online; these are often referred to as hosted data and apps.

CFO, Chief Financial Officer. The primary officer of a corporation responsible for managing the corporation's finances.

CIO, Chief Information Officer. The primary officer of a corporation responsible for managing all of the corporation's technology. This position is also often referred to as the CTO, or Chief Technology Officer.

COO, Chief Operations Officer. The primary officer of a corporation responsible for managing the corporation's day-to-day operations.

CTO, Chief Technology Officer. The primary officer of a corporation responsible for managing all of the corporation's technology. This position is also often referred to as the CIO, or Chief Information Officer.

D

Datacenter. Any place that has servers can be referred to as a datacenter. However, the term usually refers to a location that is very large and houses thousands of servers.

DRP, Disaster Recovery Plan. A detailed plan of how an organization will recover from a disaster.

DNS, Domain Name System. The worldwide system that facilitates internet connectivity by storing data about how to connect to every website, email server, and so on.

E

Encryption. A technological scrambling of data that requires a digital key to unscramble and access encrypted data. The key is provided by running an app, whether it's part of the operating system or independent of the operating system.

ESXi. VMware's hypervisor.

F

Firewall. A hardware or software solution to keep intruders out of a computer system.

G

GUI, Graphical User Interface. The presentation by an app of its features and data on a computer monitor or display; how a computer user interfaces with the computer app.

H

Hardware. Physical computers and other IT infrastructure devices.

Hosted. The location of the servers, data, and apps; hosted usually refers to an off-site location, though when located in-house it can be referred to as *locally hosted*.

HyperV. Microsoft's hypervisor.

Hypervisor. An app that allows a physical computer to be configured as a host of multiple virtual computers.

I

Infrastructure. Like roads and utilities are part of a geographic region's infrastructure, the servers, switches, and cabling that facilitate the access and sharing of data are called IT infrastructure.

Insource. Hiring employees to do tasks because the tasks are an organization's mission or core skill set.

ISO. A file that is an image of a CD or DVD that can be mounted logically just as though it was physical media. You can also burn an iso file to optical media and run it that way.

IT, Information Technology. The profession and application of computers to store, recall, transmit, and manipulate data in an organization.

L

LAN, Local Area Network. A connected group of computers and devices at an organization, usually located at the organization's site.

Licensing. The terms of the legal permission that gives the purchaser of apps and hardware the right to use their purchase within certain limits and sometimes with certain restrictions.

Live Attendant. An internal telephone system's receptionist or operator that is a live person.

Local Admin. A desktop or notebook computer setting that gives the person using it the ability to make modifications, like adding an app. This capability sometimes is reserved only for the professional IT staff. Local Admin rights do not impact a user's network rights or permissions.

M

Malware. Apps that are written for the express purpose of destroying data and systems, or holding them captive for ransom.

MBS, Ministry Business Services, Inc. The IT consulting firm founded by the author, Nick Nicholaou. (*www.mbsinc.com*)

Mission Critical. Something that, if it fails, will result in the failure of the organization's operations.

N

NAS, Network Attached Storage. A server-type device on a network that provides storage, acting like an external hard drive. NAS servers predate SANs, and provide file-level access to their contents.

NOS, Network Operating System. Similar to the operating system on a computer, this operating system is what makes it possible for the computer to function as a server on a network server vs a regular computer.

O

Outsource. Hiring non-employees to do tasks that are not an organization's mission or core skill set.

OS, Operating System. Every computer and device runs a foundational software that enables it to run apps and meet the needs of its user. Examples are Windows, Mac OSX, Android, and iOS.

P

PBX, Private Branch Exchange. Internal telephone systems typified by a central operator or receptionist.

Private Cloud. Cloud-based servers and services only accessible to those who were pre-approved to access and use them.

Productivity Software. A set of apps that usually includes word processing, spreadsheets, and other modules.

Public Cloud. Cloud-based servers and services accessible to any who would like to connect to them, such as Facebook, Dropbox, Instagram, and so on.

S

SAN, Storage Area Network. Similar to a NAS, a SAN is a server-like device that is like a large external hard drive that network users can access. It has more redundancy and safety built into it than a NAS, and is faster. SANs' contents are at the block level vs. the file level, thus requiring a server or some kind of client to access the files stored on them.

Softphone. An app that replaces the physical telephone handset.

Software. The applications used on computers to accomplish tasks, also referred to as apps.

SSID, Service Set Identifier. The name of the WiFi signals available to connect a device to.

SYOM, Spend Your Own Money. One of the BYOD strategies in which church team members contribute to the cost of their computers or mobile devices.

V

Virtual Host. A server-class physical computer that has a hypervisor installed, allowing it to host multiple virtual (non-physical) servers.

Virtualization. Computers that are not actual physical computers but are virtual configurations that act like separate computers made possible by an app referred to as a hypervisor.

VoIP, Voice over Internet Protocol. Telephone systems that transmit calls using internet technology rather than traditional telephone technology.

VPN, Virtual Private Network. A secure method of accessing data, usually from off-site, that involves encrypting the communication signal.

W

WAP, Wireless Access Point. The WiFi radios that broadcast WiFi signals.

X

XenServer. Citrix's hypervisor.

TABLE OF REFERENCES

This is a list of people and ministries who were quoted or referenced through this book.

ABOUT THE AUTHOR

Nick Bruce Nicholaou grew up in an agnostic home and is the oldest of three and the only son of a couple that began their marriage very young. He chose a childhood path that destined him to an early grave, and he would have ended up there if the Lord had not gotten his attention at the age of twenty-one.

When God got a hold of his life, he gave Nick a thirst and hunger for the Scriptures and tied him to a group of believers who helped shape his desire to serve God in every way possible—however the Lord wanted.

After college, Nick was hired into executive service in the automobile manufacturing industry where he was tasked to help dealerships improve their customer satisfaction and success. Because he had to influence independent business owners to change some of what they did and how they did it, the Lord used that time to develop Nick's consulting skills.

Just months into his marriage, while in devotions one day, Nick sensed the Lord telling him he wanted Nick to do something different. *This must be the result of last night's pepperoni*, Nick thought. But then it happened the next two days also! So, Nick decided he needed to tell his wife, Grace, even though she might think him weird. She responded, "I've been getting the *same thing!*" So they determined to discover what that meant by researching the needs of churches and how the Lord might use them to help meet those needs.

Their sense was that he wanted to take Nick's business management skills and Grace's accounting skills (she's a CPA who has focused her practice on serving Christian churches and ministries) and use them to help Christian churches and ministries across the United States. That was in 1986. They have been fulfilling that call ever since!

When Nick was in college—before the advent of the personal computer—he believed computers could be great tools to help accomplish many tasks better and more efficiently. While majoring in business administration with a management focus, he took a computer course every semester so he could gain access to the school's mainframe computer system.

Nick often says that it is amazing what God can do with someone who is willing and available to serve him, however he wants! And, that he, himself, is proof!

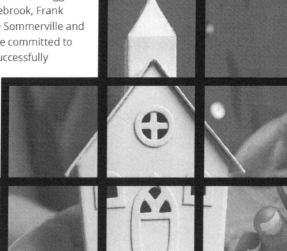

60656312R00085

Made in the USA
Lexington, KY
14 February 2017